GROTIUS' UNIVERSE

Divine Law and
a Quest for Harmony

Manufactured in the United States of America

Library of Congress Catalog Card No.: 76-19975

Standard Book Number 533-02274-6

ISBN: 1493501704

ISBN 13: 9781493501700

To the memory of my brother, Miodrag
and of my parents,
Ljubica and Lt. Colonel Milan V. Sotirovich, K.S., M. C..

GROTIUS' UNIVERSE

Divine Law and a Quest for Harmony

by

William Vasilio Sotirovich

Table of Contents

PREFACE TO THE FIRST EDITION

Grotius' Universe: A Quest for Harmony emphasizes the political philosopher and the theologian in Hugo Grotius and thus provides an additional dimension to his genius. His understanding of the world was that of a design for universal harmony whose realization was conditioned on the positive relationship between man and his creator. Numerous scholars and jurists have written about Hugo Grotius as the founder of international law and indeed his importance in this respect remains unquestionable. But Grotius was much more than a jurist. He contributed to almost every field of thought, his work extending from law and ethics to philosophy, theology, politics and international organization. He was also a man of action, a magistrate, a diplomat, and a statesman. Grotius, who belongs to the era of the Reformation and the Renaissance, was also one of the founders of modern political thought and represents not the break but the transition from medieval to modern political philosophy. In this interpretation, I have tried to point out that Grotius was able to synthesize what we now call the classical, the medieval, and the modern strains of the tradition of contemporary political philosophy.

Grotius has been glorified for his *opus magnum De Jure Belli ac Pacis* (*On the Law of War and Peace*). While the greatness of this work cannot be disputed, another perhaps less known work of Grotius is *De Veritate Religionis Christianae* (*On the Truth of Christian Religion*). In fact, the total Grotius can be fully understood if the whole product of his philosophical, juridic, and theological genius is considered as a continuum on which *De Jure* and *De Veritate* stand not in juxtaposition but are complementary with each other. Thus the theological and the juridic thought and discourse of Grotius are in perfect harmony.

This work was completed at the University of Chicago and submitted as a Master of Arts dissertation to the University of Chicago Federated Theological faculty under the title, *Divine Law in the Main Works of Hugo Grotius*. My gratitude goes to Professor of Ethics and Society Dr. Alvin Pitcher, who in 1957 read the manuscript and made valuable suggestions for the completion of this work. I am equally grateful to the Very Rev. Harold J. Buxton, Bishop of Gibraltar; to the Rev. Dr. Dimitrije Najdanovich, Principal of Dorchester College; to Dr. J. N. D. Kelly, Principal of St. Edmund Hall, Oxford; to Dr. Cynthia Wedel, president of the National Council of Churches; and to Dr. Ray Jurjevich of the Department of Clinical Psychology at the University of Denver. Their ecumenical enthusiasm, contributions to scholarship, and work on Christian Unity served as an impetus for undertaking this study.

However, the final encouragement for the publication of *Grotius' Universe* came from my wife Moira who, being a devoted physician, felt that a healthy commonwealth of nations would be better sustained if the ideas and thoughts of a genius like Hugo Grotius became widely known and thoroughly understood. Alongside such encouragement, Moira, as well as my niece Liliana, helped out with the revision and the proofreading of the manuscript. To both I owe my gratitude. Finally, I should like to record my special thanks to my wife Moira for completing the index to this book.

Our conviction is that this interpretation of Grotius and the recently renewed interest among the scholars and academicians in political philosophy may bring about further study of his writings. A new look into Hugo Grotius is not only necessary but definitely important. This is particularly true if we consider that the search for stability and the quest for harmony in the changing world of today still remains the primary consideration of mankind.

W.V.S.
N.Y.C., 1977

PREFACE TO THE SECOND EDITION

This second edition of *Grotius' Universe: Divine Law and a Quest for Harmony* is being published as a reminder of the year 1583 when Hugo Grotius, famous Dutch jurist known as the father of International Law, was born in Delft, present day Netherlands. During his life and even in his early youth, he made enormous contributions to many fields of human knowledge from poetry and literature to ethics, theology, and philosophy, to science and history, and especially to the field of law and jurisprudence. Notably, he admired astronomy and ancient Greek philosophy. To wit, in 1600, Grotius published *Aratea*, his version of Aratus' *Phaenomena*, which was originally published in 1499.[1]

Grotius' contributions to the fields of inquiry mentioned above have been properly acknowledged by hundreds of philosophers and intellectuals who wrote books and articles about, and commentaries on, his thoughts, ideas, and evaluations of various aspects of human knowledge and activities both in private and public life. International law societies, university professorships, scientific journals, and yearly conferences on international law have been established and held in his name. These tributes continue in our own century.

Grotius' Universe is a modest analysis of the interrelationship between theology and jurisprudence in the works of the Dutch philosopher and public intellectual; thus, his work is a topic that has been of interest to the students of his writings. It is therefore gratifying to this author to know that several contemporary scholars and teachers of international law and history have read and commented on *Grotius' Universe*. Among these we can include late Yale University Professor Emeritus Myres MacDougal, who was well known for teaching many domestic and foreign statesmen and for publishing numerous works in jurisprudence, including *Law and Public Order in Space*.[2] Professor MacDougal is also known for having presided over The International Law and Grotius Heritage Commemorative Colloquium in April, 1983, at the Hague in the Netherlands.

As a well-known educator, MacDougal left his mark on many law schools and universities worldwide as well as on numerous professors of legal studies, many of whom have acknowledged *Grotius' Universe* as a valuable analysis of the philosopher-statesman's work. Professor Frederick Chen notes that Grotius was an important legal expert who studied the relationship between religion and international law,[3] while law professor Alan Karabus, when reading this book, pointed out that for almost 150 years Grotius' works influenced both the legal system and legal studies in South Africa, especially during the heyday of Dutch rule in that part of the world.

Another great educator, the late Sarah Lawrence University Professor Emeritus Adda Bozeman, personally complimented this author after reading *Grotius' Universe*. She herself admired Grotius both as a great theologian and as one of the founders of international law. She praised him in her article "On the Relevance of Hugo Grotius and *De Jure Belli ac Pacis* for our Times."[4] Similarly, one of the representatives in the League of Nations and later law professor Dr. Ivan Soubbotitch[5] wrote that the interrelationship between jurisprudence and theological studies as outlined by Grotius needed to be emphasized, as is clearly shown in *Grotius' Universe*. Finally, most recently, in his article "The Miracle of Holland," William Greene[6] composed a study of

Natural Law and its origins over many centuries, one of the main foci in Grotius' writings. In it, Greene emphasizes the importance of *Grotius' Universe* for understanding the intellectual and public statesman's explanation of the dogma of Natural Law.

It is also satisfying that *Grotius' Universe* has been quoted in articles and blogs written in Chinese[7] and in the works of students in Russian universities.

Most recently, *Grotius' Universe* has attracted the attention of prominent scholars who have suggested that even after more than 450 years, Grotius' thought and works remain important for both jurisprudence and theology. Specifically, the Very Rev. Dr. Robert Stephanopoulos, Dean Emeritus of the Greek Orthodox Cathedral in New York City, commented on how this book emphasizes that for Grotius, ecumenism and the unity of Christianity were achievable goals, an ideal that is realizable even in the current century. Similarly, another reader of *Grotius' Universe*, United States Navy chaplain Rev. Wilfredo Rodriguez, working with servicemen at the American base in Kandahar, Afghanistan, finds the book valuable for our heroic men serving the country for the purpose of establishing peace — the same objective Grotius hoped to achieve during his time.

However, most satisfying for this author is to be able to repeat that if anything else, Grotius was a realist as well as an idealist. He insisted that the human race could prosper by progressing from conflicts and disagreements between numerous nations of the world, towards greater understanding and harmony in the international relations among many states in the global system of the twenty-first century.

The existing body for furthering this movement from conflict into harmony functioning in our day and age is *The United Nations*. It is indeed appropriate to reiterate Grotius' ideas, as I explain in the conclusion of *Grotius' Universe*:

With his law of peace, he (Grotius) presented to the world the ideal conception of a family of nations

united under sovereignty of God, in a commonwealth of mankind. Thus Grotius must be regarded
as one of chief expounders of the basic ideals that
are contained in the documents like the League of
Nations Covenant, the United Nations Charter, and
the United Nations Declaration of Human Rights.

It is hoped that the second edition of *Grotius' Universe*
reaches those scholars and statesmen who still consider that
these important documents are now and will be of greatest
value for creating peace and harmony for our planet Earth
not only in this decade but in many more decades to come.

A brief biography of Hugo Grotius has been added to the
book's second edition; in addition, the book includes several images of the statesman and covers of his now-famous
texts, as well as an updated bibliography of selected books
and articles. Slight modifications have also been made to the
text of the First Edition in the form of error correction and
stylistic continuity.

To complete this publication, the author is indebted to
his wife and dedicated physician Moira Franklin-Sotirovich,
who provided constant encouragement. Similar apprecia-
tion is hereby given to Professor Jami Carlacio, who performed additional research and edited the text in order to
complete the project.

W.V.S.
N.Y.C. , 2013

NOTES

1. Grotius' work on astronomy was the direct result of his acquisition of the ninth century manuscript of Aratus, which included paintings of Aquarius, Andromeda, and Cassiopeia. Grotius had the paintings converted to engravings, which survive today and are housed at Reijksuniversitet in Leiden. See the website entitled *Linda Hall Library of Science, Engineering, and Technology.*

2. See Myres MacDougal, Harold Dwight Lasswell, and Ivan A. Vlasic, *Law and Public Order in Space,* (New Haven: Yale University Press, 1963) and Myres MacDougal, *The Public Order of the Oceans: A Contemporary International Law of the Sea* (New Haven: Yale University Press, 1962).

3. See Frederick Tse-shyang Chen, "The Confucian View of World Order," in Mark W. Janis, ed., *The Influence of Religion on the Development of International Law,* (Dordrecht: Martius Nijhoff, 1991): 38.

4. See Adda Bozeman, "On the Relevance of Hugo Grotius and *De Jure Belli ac Pacis* for our Times," *Grotiana* 1, no. 1 (1980).

5. See Walter Lipgens and Wilfried Loth, *Documents on the History of European Integration: Plans for European Union in Great Britain and in Exile, 1939-1945,* (Berlin: DeGruyter, 1985): 756.

6. See William Greene, "The Miracle of Holland: Hugo Grotius: Naturalist, Eclectic, or Theonomist?" *The Preterist Archive*, March 30, 2005.

7. See for example "The Father of Modern International Law: Grotius' Law and Human Law of God." [Translated from Chinese to English by Google Translate]. 30 June 2013.

INTRODUCTION

This interpretation of the famous Dutch theologian and lawyer Hugo Grotius was undertaken in order to indicate the relationship between theology and law in his main works. Although Grotius sincerely hoped to make a contribution to Christian thought, he achieved worldwide fame as an international lawyer. In fact, the tendency of the interpreters of Grotius has been to separate Grotius the theologian from Grotius the lawyer, and to study one or the other separately.

In this work, I have endeavored to present the relationship of Grotius the theologian to Grotius the lawyer. I have found that this relationship is very marked. The fact is that he worked in both fields at the same time and that he never abandoned his Christian convictions when dealing with law. Although his intention was to treat law as a science independent of contemporary religious opinions, his basic presuppositions rested on his Christian beliefs. He explored the writings of Greek and Roman philosophers, diligently studied "the Holy Writ," thoroughly examined the canons of the church, and used them as well as the works of the prominent Christian writers. The completion of this task resulted in a synthesis of the ideas found in these sources.

The main intention of Grotius was to deal with the philosophy of law. For this purpose, he employed his new system of ethics. From it, he developed the law of mankind, which should be freely accepted and observed by all men and by all nations. This law of mankind has its origin in Divine law. Its underlying ethical precepts have the power of directing and not commanding. From its rules, Grotius deduced the precepts for what may rightly be called the new international ethics.

Grotius remained in the tradition of natural law theory, but his main significance consists in his giving to that body of moral precepts a new interpretation. His thought is important for theology and for philosophy. As for the first, it is right to say that he pointed to what may rightly be called the Christian theory of law. He divided Divine law into its constituent parts. I use the terms the "true law of nature," "Divine Positive law," and "Natural law" to describe these parts.

As for the second, Grotius gave the impetus for the development of the modern theory of natural law. Writing at the dawn of the new age of science, he used the scientific method for the analysis of law. By separating the Christian from purely rationalist elements in the medieval interpretation of the law of nature theory, he defined two areas covered by the law of nature. I use the terms "the law of nature" and "natural law"; the former term applies to the laws of science, the latter to laws governing man's moral actions. For the rationalists, human reason is sufficient for the discovery of the norms of these two laws, but, for Grotius, man cannot achieve a deeper understanding of these laws without the law of Christ.

I have found that in his works, Grotius emphasizes the importance of Divine Positive law. In his system, this law holds the whole structure of law together. Grotius indicates that the approach of man to Divine law is made possible through Christ, in whom God and man, and therefore Divine and human reason, are perfectly united. Thus, Divine Positive law appears as the irremovable link between Divine law and man's understanding of that law.

For Grotius, the law of Christ is equal to the law of mankind, that is to say, the law of Christ prescribes ethical precepts for all nations. Grotius refers to this law as the law of nations.

Distinction must be made between this law and the written laws of nations, which is the product of human will. This law incorporates the *ius gentium*, and the customs, agreements, and pacts established mostly before the Christian era.

For the main positive human laws, Grotius used the terms "municipal (state) law" and "the law of nations." Both are defined in statutes, the former binding on the citizens of a state, the latter binding on smaller or larger groups of states. Grotius tried to evaluate these human laws from the standpoint of the law of mankind.

From what has been said above, it follows that natural theology and rational morality are not the only content of the religion of Grotius. The spirit of his works and the constant reference to the immanence of God in the world indicate the strong Christian beliefs of this author. Therefore, I have made an effort to show that Grotius was as far from deism as Christianity itself is far from it.

In short, this study rests on three arguments: first, that Grotius created a new international ethic; second, that he redefined the theory of natural law; and third, that he was a Christian and cannot be classed as a deist. These three arguments suffice to show that his theological thought strongly influenced his works in the field of law.

Chapter I is mainly concerned with Divine law and its three constituent parts. I show the relationship between the true law of nature and the Divine Positive law. According to Grotius, the true understanding of the two by man results in a better understanding of Natural law.

Chapter II deals with what may be called the natural theology of Grotius. In Christian terminology, this is called the Unrevealed Divine law. To the classical interpreters of natural law, the constitution of the universe leads human reason to the idea of a hidden Supreme Being. According to this view, both natural law and the law of nature could be discovered by the simple process of observation of man and nature surrounding him.

Chapter III is concerned with the Revealed Divine law. The name employed for this law in the work is "Divine Positive law." Grotius used both the Old and the New Testaments to present the express commands of God, which reveal His will.

Finally, in Chapters IV and V, I endeavor to show how the blending of the two first laws produces the law of mankind. Grotius applied Divine law to different human situations. Divine law, to which the name "law of mankind" is given, ought to direct the actions of man: first, as an individual; second, as a member of an individual state; and third, through the state as a member of the commonwealth of mankind.

Before I begin the exposition of Grotius' works, two qualifications must be made: first, considering that Grotius wrote more than three centuries ago, a good deal of his views can be discarded as not applicable anymore. This remark especially applies to his biblical criticism, to his views on the divine right of kings, on the question of slavery, rules of postliminy, etc.

Second, in spite of these shortcomings, the main body of the apologetic work of Grotius, his exposition of the Christian ethic, and his principles of international theory, still remain valid. However, for the presentation of these elements of the apologetics, ethics, and theory of Grotius, I had to employ a number of terms, in order to define, at least approximately, different ideas in the system of Grotius. A list of these terms follows the conclusion.

A Biographical Sketch[2]

Often called "Father of International Law," the famous Dutch jurist Hugo Grotius (Huig de Groot, Hugo Grocio, and Hugo de Groot [1583-1645]), was, along with his contemporaries Francisco de Vitoria and Alberto Gentili, most certainly one of its founders. Born in Delft, Holland, to Jan de Groot and Alida van Overschie, his early childhood is compared to that of Swedish diplomat and former United Nations Secretary-General Dag Hammarskjöld,[1] since both were steeped in a long tradition of public service and received a deeply religious education—a dual heritage clearly evident not only in their lives but also in their activities.

A child prodigy, Grotius was provided with a classical education; in his early youth, he became an expert in Greek and Latin. The young Grotius not only studied these languages but also diligently reproduced several ancient writings. For example, fascinated by the celestial marvels of the universe, the seventeen-year-old Grotius published the studies of the third century B.C.E. Greek poet and astronomer Solensis Aratus in a work titled *Syntagma Arataeorum*.

Previous to this, at age fifteen, Grotius graduated from the University of Leiden and then accompanied the Dutch statesman Johan van Oldenbarnevelt on a mission to France. Here he earned a doctoral degree from the University of Orleans; subsequently, he was presented to an impressed King Henry IV. On his return to Holland, Grotius accomplished many things, including the publication of a work by Martianus Capella, which addressed the seven liberal arts: *Martiani Minei Felicis Capellae Carthaginiensis Viri Proconsularis Satyricon, in quo de Nuptiis Philogiae et Mercurij Libri Duo, et de Septem Artibus Liberalibus Libri Singulares. Omnes, et emendati, et notis, siue Februis Hug. Grotii illustrati.*

Not yet twenty years of age, in 1601 Grotius became a historiographer for the state of Holland; in due time he produced several works: *Liber de Antiquitate Republicae Batavicae, auctore Hugone Grotio, Lugduni Batavorum* and *Annales et Historiae de Rebus Belgicis, Amstelaedami.* Subsequently, he published important work on jurisprudence, whose influence lasted several centuries both in Holland and in South Africa: *Inleydinge tot de Hollandsche Rechts-geleertheit, beschreven bij Hugo de Groot Part 1* (*Introduction to the Jurisprudence of Holland, described by Hugo de Groot*).

While working on these studies, Grotius was appointed in 1604 as legal councilor to the Prince of Orange, Mauritius (Maurice) von Nassau. In 1607, he was appointed Attorney General for the Courts of Holland and later became both the Governor of Rotterdam and Attorney General of the United Netherlands.

At about the same time, he assumed the role of legal advisor to the Dutch East India Company; soon after, he became embroiled in a complicated legal controversy. While the Dutch had built a strong navy and maintained a considerable role in sea-trade, they necessarily competed with Spain, Portugal, and England, three countries that persisted in monopolizing the seas. When in 1605 a Dutch ship attacked the Portuguese vessel Santa Catarina in the waters of the East Indies and captured its cargo, Grotius defended the action, publishing his famous *Mare Liberum* (*Freedom of the Sea*), in which he argued that trade and communications among nations of the world must be the right and privilege of everybody, and that the principle of freedom of the sea did not allow for a monopoly of the oceans by any specific nation in the world. *Mare Liberum* brought fame to Grotius and was translated into many languages. It was considered to be the most important statement by an authority in the law of nations.

These early years of the unusually successful life of young Hugo Grotius were also ones of tremendous changes in Europe. For example, Holland and all of the provinces of the Spanish possessions in the Netherlands were fighting for independence; the conflict between Roman Catholicism and Protestantism was in full force; and the entire European continent was heavily engaged in the Thirty Years War. In addition to these conflicts, the Dutch people were confronted with challenges of their own. As a religious population, they entered into a phase of conflict in theological orientation. Primarily followers of Calvinism, a great number seemed to disagree over one's dedication to important religious doctrines. Two branches emerged, one becoming followers of the teachings of Franciscus Gomarus and the other, the teachings of Jacobus Arminius. This split produced a strongly divided church population. The former strictly emphasized the Calvinist doctrine of predestination whereas the latter stressed free will.

Given Grotius' public service and his own strong sense of religious orientation, it was perhaps inevitable that he would become intimately involved in this religious controversy. As a member of the Committee of Councilors under the Armenian Party led by van Oldenbarnevelt, Grotius took an active role in the Arminian-oriented States General, which opposed the strictly Calvinist-oriented Holland. He made his position clear in his theological writings, first in 1613 with *Pietas Ordinum Hollandiae ac Westfrisiae Vindicata* and in 1614 with *Bona Fides Sibrandi Lubberti*. He continued with his arguments in his dissertation, *De Imperio Summarum Potestum Circa Sacra*.

By the second decade of the seventeenth century this religious controversy became violent. Grotius worked closely with his childhood friend and collaborator Prime Minister van Oldenbarnevelt, who was confronted by the Prince of Orange, von Nassau. In 1618, after a short battle between the two opposing parties, the forces behind the Prince of Orange overwhelmed those of van Oldenbarnevelt. The latter was captured and after a short trial condemned for treason. The Arminians were defeated and van Oldenbarnevelt suffered the death sentence. Grotius, his strong supporter, narrowly avoided similar sentence, but was nevertheless condemned to life imprisonment without parole.

Though secluded in the Castle Loevestein and thus separated from his allies, Grotius was allowed to continue with his scholarly work. He had access to numerous books, wrote prolifically, and enjoyed frequent visits by his wife, Maria van Reigersberg. Despite his life sentence, which would certainly seem to have ended the statesman's brilliant career,

Grotius was able to produce the outline for the book that was eventually published posthumously: the famous *De Jure Praedae Commentarius*, whose twelfth chapter was the glorious *Mare Liberum*.

Studious as ever, Grotius continued with his work, outlining the many theological writings that were formulated many years later. His concentration on the Bible produced many ideas for further work, but it did not stop him from writing poetry and historical dramas. Moreover, his total immersion in literary pursuits did not mean that Grotius would cease his search for freedom and escape from captivity. His wife Maria, a competent and courageous person, together with others, eventually helped Grotius break from prison in 1621 by hiding him in a wooden case designed to transport books and then carrying it out of Loevestein Castle.

Grotius managed to flee to Amsterdam and soon afterwards to Paris, where King of France Louis XIII provided him not only with refuge but also with a permanent income, which enabled the freed prisoner to bring his family to join him in his new home. Living in France proved to be important insofar as Grotius was able to continue his legal and religious scholarship as well as his literary pursuits.

Within a few years of arrival in France, Grotius produced many of the Biblical studies that were later published as *Hugonis Grotii Annotationes in Libros Evangeliorum cum Tribus Tractatibus* (*Annotationum in Novum Testamentum Tomus I*); *Hugonis Grotii Annotationes in Novum Testamentum Tomus Secundus* (*Annotationes in Acta Apostolorum et Epistolas Apostolicas*); *Hugonis Grotii Annotata ad Vetus Testamentum, Tomus I (III)*; and *Lutetiae Parisiorum* (sumtibus Sebastiani Cramoisi et Gabrielis Cramoisy).

Grotius also published poetry and drama during this time; his expertise in Greek and Latin enabled him to produce *Dicta Poetarum quae apud Io. Stobaeum Exstant Emendata et Latino Carmine reddita ab Hugone Grotio,* and *Exerpta ex Tragoediis et Comoediis Graeciis tum quae Exstant tum quae*

Perierunt, Emendata et Latinis Versibus reddita ab Hugone Grotio. Notably, he published a dissertation on the newly discovered American continent: *Hugonis Grotii De Origine Americanarum.*

Notwithstanding his literary accomplishments, Grotius' most famous work produced while living in France was *De Jure Belli ac Pacis Libri Tres, in Quibus ius Naturae et Gentium, Iuris Publici Praecipus Explicandur.* Published in Paris in 1625, this supreme elaboration on the theory of "just war" brought fame to the scholar and secured his place in history as the true founder of international law and genius in the field of jurisprudence. Over the years, *De Jure Belli ac Pacis* was republished many times and in many languages; to this day it remains a classic. In this enormous three-volume work, Grotius details the relationship among different nations in the global system, insisting that actions and goals of world leaders and of people in general must move toward establishing justice, protecting rights, and punishing wrongs. If most nations and all states were to work along these lines, Grotius argued, there would be no wars and the world would experience peace and security.

At the same time, aware of the nature of human weakness and of men's inability to arrive at a state of perfection, Grotius allowed for conflict and disagreement between states, which would conceivably result in serious confrontations, including war. In discussing war as "unnecessary evil," he does not refute its existence but advocates three different methods for their solution and termination. First, states engaged in conflict should participate in conferences and negotiations in order to end war; second, the parties should seek compromise, with each being willing to concede certain demands and to make due concessions; third, if neither of the two positive solutions can be achieved, then combat for the sake of justice and peace is totally acceptable. He admitted, that is, that there may be instances in which "just war" would be necessary.

In addition to publishing *De Jure Belli ac Pacis*, Grotius also completed his famous *De Veritate Religionis Christianae*, which was published in Paris in 1627. The book's purpose was to serve the sailors confronting Jews, Muslims, heathens, and atheists in their worldwide voyages. These two major publications secured Grotius' fame throughout Europe and were translated into several languages.

The year 1631 proved to be a turning point in Grotius' life. The new governing leadership of Holland allowed for many Dutch exiles to return to their native country. Prince Frederick Henry, son of William of Orange, became the undisputed ruler; he was, in fact, a good friend of Grotius since their days as students at Leiden University many years previous. Encouraged by Prince Frederick, Grotius decided to return to Holland, settling in Amsterdam, where he resumed his law practice. He was even offered the governorship of the Dutch East India Company. Despite this promising turn of events, in order to remain in his own country and to maintain his well-established position, Grotius was obligated to apologize and repent for his previous opposition to the old regime. Grotius refused to comply with these demands and thus found himself in a difficult position. He was soon forced to go into exile again. This time, Grotius settled temporarily in Hamburg, Germany.

Despite the fact that political circumstances forced Grotius to live away from the country of his birth, where he had established his career, his reputation for his literary achievements and his scholarly work on jurisprudence spread throughout the continental Europe. Deemed a leading scholar and a man of great integrity, he had earned the respect of many prominent people, including the King of Sweden, who kept a copy of *De Jure Belli ac Pacis* with him when he traveled. In 1634, the Swedish king appointed Hugo Grotius as Swedish Ambassador to France, and it was during his tenure as ambassador that he represented Sweden in treaty negotiations that led, in 1648, to the end of the Thirty Years War in Westphalia.

In addition to his ambassadorial duties, he continued his scholarly pursuits, this time writing on legal matters and analyzing many histories of European development: *Historia Gottorum, Vandalorum et Langobardorum ab Hugone Grotio, Partim Versa, Partim in Ordinem Digesta, Auctorum Ordinem Indicat*. This was followed by two other studies: *Batavi, Parallelon Rerum publicarum Liber Tertius* (4 volumes) and *Leges Barbarorum*: the *Lex Wisigothorum* and the *Edictum Theoderici*. He also became interested in the history of the Byzantine Empire, which resulted in the publication of *Florum Sparsio ad ius Iustinianum*.

Eventually, in 1645, Grotius was released from his post as Swedish ambassador to France by Count Axel Oxenstierna. Soon after, he was offered a new job in Sweden's capital of Stockholm, working with its new ruler, Queen Christina. Anxious to start his new assignment and keen to meet with the queen, Grotius traveled in early March by boat across the stormy waters of the Baltic Sea to Stockholm. The turbulent waters caused the boat to capsize, and though Grotius barely survived this shipwreck, he persisted in his goal to return to Sweden. That summer, the boat on which he was traveling met with disaster on the shores of Germany; seeming initially to have survived this shipwreck, Grotius died several days later in Rostock, Germany, on August 28th, 1645.

Certainly, Grotius' influence in International Law deserves the worldwide recognition it has received over the last four centuries. At the same time, his impact on the poetry and literature of other famous poets cannot go unnoticed. For example, his 1601 publication of *Sacra in Quibus Adamus Exul Tragoedia Aliorumque Eiusdem Generis Carminum Cumulus*, later known as *Adamus Exul* or *Expulsion of Adame and Eva from Paradise*, fascinated the British poet John Milton, who used it as the basis and prototype of his epic, *Paradise Lost*. This poem's publication in 1667 secured for Milton a place in history as one of the world's greatest poets of his time.

Just as Grotius' literary achievements influenced others who achieved a similarly high stature in their creative pursuits, his work in politics and in political philosophy influenced major thinkers such as Britain's John Locke, author of the famous *Two Treatises of Civil Government*, published in 1689. This significant discourse on socio-political governance influenced the Founding Fathers of America, who produced the *Declaration of Independence* and the *United States Constitution*.

Grotius' influence on religion also lives on, particularly due to his role in the religious controversies that occurred between the Gomarists and Arminians, which resulted in a life sentence for him 1618. His work has survived through the theological doctrines of Jacob Arminius (1560-1609). Arminianism, whose doctrine promotes the belief that every person is entitled to God's grace and to freedom of human will, ran counter to the Calvinist belief in predestination. Arminianism was integral to Grotius' theological philosophy and writing, which survives to this day. In fact, its tenets became the inspiration for the teachings of John Wesley, who established the new Methodist Church. In its missionary zeal, Methodism spread everywhere in the British Empire as well as in North and South America. Today, the Methodist Church, an indirect product of the teachings of Arminius and Grotius, has a membership of nearly eighty million adherents throughout the world, including the famous American evangelist Billy Graham.

The life of Hugo Grotius ended tragically in a small seaside town in Germany; years after, his remains were buried in Delft. A great and influential statesman, legal scholar, theologian and poet, he passed away without witnessing the reconciliation if not the reunification of all followers of Christianity — an ideal he strove for most of his life to achieve.

NOTES

1. Dag Hammarskjöld served as the second Secretary-General of the UN from April 1953 to September 1961, when he was killed in a plane crash on the way to cease-fire negotiations.

2. Much of the background information in this section has been adapted from "Hugo Grotius," *Wikipedia.* Copyright Creative Commons Attribution-ShareAlike license.

CHAPTER 1:

DIVINE OR NATURAL LAW

The Origin and Development of Law

The work of Grotius was that of a genius, considering the task he set before himself, namely, to present the whole body of law, to dissect it, and to analyze its parts in order to show the relationship of the separate units to the whole. He visualized the body of law as an organic unit, but with separate functions, and conducted a survey of its anatomy with scientific precision. He did this not in order to dispose of any of its parts,[1] but, on the contrary, in order to preserve the unity of the law, whose separate members are indispensable to one another. If any of the subsystems of the law are removed, coordination and balance is lost, and the whole system is bound to collapse. The division of law into its component parts is commendable for the sake of analysis, but one part cannot be fully understood except in its relationship to the other.

The systematic presentation of Grotius has these underlying axioms: God is the possessor of Divine Will and of Divine Reason; He is the Creator of the universe; He is the

1

Creator of man, of human will, and of human reason. The dynamism of God's Being is exemplified in three ways. By the fact of God's Creativity, He is the Author of the laws that govern nature and of all created matter, including man. His Will directs the development of that matter and directs the actions of man. His Reason serves as the directing and uniting power of His Creativity and of His Will.

These three manifestations of God are seen by men through the three laws which constantly emanate from God: the true law of nature, parts of which men are capable of discovering; the Divine Positive law, which men should follow; and Natural law, to which men must adjust their actions.

Without Divine Positive law, it would seem that the two entities, God, on the one side, and man, on the other side, could exist separately. This would be the rationalist position, according to which Nature's God could replace the immanent Christian God. However, Grotius saw the situation differently. For him, God was immanent as well as transcendent. The dynamic movement in the universe was in fact the result of the dynamic power which emanates from God. Everything that was created and is being created acts in accordance with harmony and unity. In other words, the existence of perfect order has always been the result of God's presence everywhere. His active participation and care for the world maintains this order.

It must be remembered that Grotius visualized the order, harmony, and unity in the universe as the product of God's Freedom of action. On the other hand, Grotius was faced with the realities of the world, which indicated disorder, disharmony, and disunity. According to Grotius, such a state of affairs was the result of the freedom of man. This factor was, in fact, the crux of the destiny of man, since, using his freedom, man could either achieve unity with God, or could place himself in juxtaposition to God.

Mankind has experienced this process. The abuse of freedom brought about the disruption of the harmonious relationship between God and man and between man and nature. As a consequence, man was unable to understand either the true law of nature or Natural law. Divine Positive law was therefore given to men in order to serve as a guide for their faith and their reason.

Grotius did not claim that complete understanding of Divine law was possible, but he believed that natural law, the latter being the human comprehension of the former, was accessible to man. Divine law, as presented by Christ, demanded perfection, while natural law allowed for human imperfection.

A reading of Grotius suggests that human positive laws, deduced from the ethical concepts of natural law, were not always absolutely valid. They were concerned, first, with individual commonwealths (civil or municipal laws); and second, with the family of commonwealths (laws of nations). Man was subject to both, but his ultimate allegiance, according to Grotius, was always to the law of mankind.[2]

Natural Law

Grotius begins his analysis from the point of view of man as a creature in nature. Being a believer in the power of reason, he draws his conclusions from the observation of nature in general and of man's actions in particular; in this way, he arrives at the law of nature. Natural law and its true reflection in the law of nature is "the necessary order, immutable and admitting of no exceptions, to which each natural thing conforms. . . ."[3]

Here is the crucial point of Grotius' analysis. The definition may be applied to both scientific laws governing the created matter, and to moral laws governing the actions of men.

The law of nature, again, is unchangeable — even in the sense that it cannot be changed by God. . . . Sometimes nevertheless it happens that in the acts in regard to

3

which the law of nature has ordained something, an appearance of change deceives the unwary, although in fact the law of nature, being unchangeable, undergoes no change; but the thing in regard to which the law of nature has ordained, undergoes change.[4]

God, being the perfect Creator, has created perfect laws of nature to govern the universe. Thus far, it would seem that the laws of nature are static, and it may also seem that God, like man, is determined by the created matter. According to this line of thought, man would tend to pursue only his own good. However, God is also perfect Reason and perfect Will, both of which are dynamic. As such, they are Natural law, which is not subject to nature, but controls and governs it. Following these precepts, man must promote the common good. When man puts himself into a position superior to nature, he acquires an approximate comprehension of Natural law. Grotius' term "Natural law" must be taken to mean what Thomas Aquinas means by "Eternal law." Then, the definition of Grotius becomes clear. Natural law cannot be changed by God, since it has never been made.

It has not been made even by God, since it is nothing but the reason of God.[5]

Taken to mean this, Natural law and Divine Positive law are not contradictory to each other, since the Reason of God and the Will of God are in perfect harmony. On the other hand, the law of nature, taken on its own, may sometimes contradict Natural law. As pointed out earlier, this contradiction may result from man's abuse of freedom. If we assume that the law of nature is only human understanding of one of the manifestations of Divine law, then the next definition of Grotius is fully understood:

The law of nature[6] is a dictate of right reason, which points out that an act, according as it is or is not in conformity with rational nature, has in it a quality of moral baseness or moral necessity; and that, in consequence, such an act is either forbidden or enjoined by the author of nature, God.[7]

Grotius recognized two constituent elements in the reason of man: first, the natural reason of man, which is in compliance with the law of nature; this accounts for the precept of self-preservation natural to every man; and second, right or moral reason, which is in compliance with Natural law and with the Reason of God; from this source comes the precept of love and sacrifice:

> I willingly recognize the fact that in the Gospel nothing is enjoined upon us which does not have the quality of natural moral goodness; but I do not see why I should grant that we are not bound by the laws of Christ beyond the limit of obligation imposed by the law of nature of and by itself.[8]

These three statements of Grotius are not contradictory to one another, but it may be concluded from them that the law of nature, as seen by man, does not completely disclose Divine law. The two laws, one discovered by man in God's creation, and the other originating in God's Creativity, Will, and Reason, were originally meant to conform to each other. However, since a departure from the original design of God has been produced by man's freedom of action, the distorted law of nature had to be corrected by God's intervention. Grotius saw this process as the manifestation of the constant action of God.

The dynamic activity of God is at its best in the relationship of the three constitutive parts which make up the essence of Divine law. In God, all law is at its perfect unity and perfect harmony. His Creativity is directed by His Will, and both are coordinated by the power of His Reason. Love and Freedom, which are in their fullness in God's Being, lead all actions of God toward complete Goodness.

With man, the situation is different. His love is a blending of self-love and the love for others; his freedom, although complete, is not perfect. His creativity, his will, and his reason lead toward good only when freely united with God. In order to achieve his unity with God, man must submit himself to Divine laws. By the very fact of his existence, man is submitted to the law of nature; that is, he is created by God. The precepts of this law have to be qualified by the precepts of the law expressly given to man in the Divine Positive law. The proper application of the latter law to the former will result in the correct usage of human reason.[9]

Grotius says that, being subject to nature:

> . . . man is to be sure, an animal, but an animal of superior kind; he is different from other animals due to . . . the essential traits implanted in man . . . because of His [God's] having willed that such traits exist in us; . . . By means of the laws which he has given, God has made those fundamental traits more manifest . . . and He has forbidden us to yield to impulses drawing us in the opposite directions.[10]

For Grotius, the existence of the Universal Church meant the constant presence of Christ, and, therefore, the immanence of God in the world. Yet, for him, the church as a community of men did not differ from the church existing in every human being. Thus, the understanding of Natural law,[11] which comprised both the true law of nature and Divine Positive law, was equally accessible to the community and to the individual.[12]

Grotius synthesized man's understanding of the Divine laws by exploring the sources which he found in writings of ancient Greek and Roman philosophers. He constantly referred to Plato, Aristotle, Cicero, and the Stoics. However, their understanding of Natural law appeared to him inadequate. Their interpretation pointed to a God removed from the world, and to man who both conceived the laws of nature and created human laws through his reason. The interpretation of Natural law which Grotius gave was different from the original one, since Grotius relied on a much stronger source, in which the Will of God was precisely expressed.

> I frequently appeal to the authority of the books which men inspired by God have either written or approved, nevertheless with a distinction between the Old Testament and the New. There are some who urge that the Old Testament sets forth the law of nature. Without doubt they are in error, for many of its rules come from the free will of God. . . . The New Testament I use in order to explain—and this cannot be learned from any other source—what is permissible to Christians. This, however—contrary to the practice of most men—I have distinguished from the law of nature, considering it as certain that in that most holy law a greater degree of moral perfection is enjoined upon us than the law of nature, alone and by itself, would require.[13]

Grotius discovered that the best interpreter of the Divine law was the church, and he used its canons to find support for his conclusions. He also employed the writings of Chrysostom, Athanasius, Ambrose, Augustine, Aquinas, and other Christian writers. Thus, revising and synthesizing the rich treasure of the ethical ideas accumulated in the long history of the Greco-Roman and Western world, he redefined the theory of natural law in the light of Divine Positive law.

Grotius believed that every individual was capable of following Divine law, but the ability to do so was conditioned by the knowledge of both the law of nature and of the

Divine Positive law. For the first, right reason was needed; for the second, true faith. He expected that the community of mankind would enjoy order and harmony if each individual commonwealth were ruled by a prince who accepted God as his Supreme Sovereign. Thus, the ideal ruler for Grotius was the "Christian prince." His anticipation of the fact that "God takes care in the affairs of men" found its best expression in the powerful prayer at the end of his *opus magnum*:

> May God, who alone hath the power, inscribe these teachings on the hearts of those who hold sway over the Christian world. May He grant to them a mind possessing knowledge of divine and human law, and having ever before it the reflection that it hath been chosen as a servant for the rule of man, the living thing most dear to God.[14]

Controversial Statements of Grotius

There are a number of controversial statements on the basis of which Grotius may be interpreted in two different ways. They convey the idea that human reason alone is sufficient for an understanding of Divine laws. Yet, a more thorough study of his works brings the underlying spirit to the fore. The meaning of references to biblical passages becomes clear. They are significant because Grotius placed them there to serve as the final authority for human actions. To take them only as examples, similar to those quoted from Greek poets, or as a means for the embellishment[15] of the text, is wrong. Attention is also drawn to certain passages that can imply a dual meaning. If taken out of context, they may suggest that Grotius was a deist, or even an atheist. Yet, this is only one possible interpretation, and not necessarily the true one.

First, Grotius used the scientific method for the synthesis of the two laws, one found in nature, the other given by Christ. He thus created a code of ethics from which he deduced the rules and the laws for human behavior. But, as may be suggested, by doing this he did not imply the removal of God from the world. Neither did he believe that man should regard these laws as finally determined[16] or unchangeable by God. His constant repetition of the phrase, "God takes care in the affairs of men," his emphasis on miracles, and his discussion of the rewards which God will grant to those who obey His laws, just as the judgments which God passes "in this life and in the life after this," are sufficient to dispel any suggestion that Grotius was a deist. His discussion of the supernatural revelation of God through Christ, whom he calls "the King of Heaven," proves that the position of Grotius was different from that of his contemporaries who were deists. As a Christian rationalist, he believed that redemption of man comes through the Grace of God and through the mediation of Christ. This must be complemented by the free response of each individual. Grotius says that God must be obeyed, rather than man; or, in other words, right reason must submit itself to God and not to nature. Faith, or right judgment, brings natural and moral reason together.

> For the principles of the law of nature, since they are always the same, can easily be brought into a systematic form; . . . With all truthfulness I aver that, just as mathematicians treat their figures as abstracted from bodies, so in treating law I have withdrawn my mind from every particular fact.[17]

According to Grotius, faith in the revelation of God helped the moral reason of man to establish the code of ethics. This was profoundly different from the deistic 18 argument that natural reason was sufficient for the discovery of moral laws. Thus, for Grotius, God was the Omnipotent Christian God, and not Nature's God (Thomas Jefferson) or the Supreme Being of the French Revolution.[19]

In the second place, Grotius argued that the true law of nature cannot be changed, even by God. The implication here may be as follows: God has created the universe, and along with it the laws by which the universe is governed; after this, He withdrew Himself, abandoning the world.

> The law of nature, again, is unchangeable — even in the sense that it cannot be changed by God. Measureless as is the power of God, nevertheless it can be said that there are certain things over which that power does not extend; for things of which this is said are spoken only, having no sense corresponding with reality and being mutually contradictory. Just as even God, then, cannot cause that two times two should not make four, so He cannot cause that that which is intrinsically evil be not evil.[20]

It has already been explained that, for Grotius, the true law of nature was in the essence of God, and therefore un changeable. Also, assuming that this law was good, it was in no need of change. The remark of Grotius that even God cannot change what is "intrinsically evil" fits into his system, if evil is taken as the result of human freedom. It may be said, however, that, in a sense, God limited Himself by creating man free. Yet freedom was indispensable for man. Without it man could not promote the universal good and thus be the co-creator with God. At the same time, by that same freedom, man was capable of pursuing his own good only, often forgetting God and rejecting his fellowman. Grotius could not ascribe the origin of evil to God. According to him, God was aware of the existence of evil, but continued to direct man, who had to correct this divergence from Divine laws by using his freedom correctly.

In the third place, the hypothesis of Grotius that natural law was valid even without reference to God's existence made the post-Grotian rationalists forget that the rationalism of Grotius was rooted in his Christian faith.

What we have been saying would have a degree of validity even if we should concede that which can not be conceded without the utmost wickedness, that there is no God, or that the affairs of men are of no concern to Him. The very opposite of this view has been implanted in us. [21]

Stating this, Grotius, in fact, rejected atheism. He would never have conceded that a system of law could exist without God, especially if the expectation of men was that such a system be good. Yet, this hypothesis became an axiom for the writers on the philosophy of law who followed in the footsteps of Grotius. [22]

NOTES

1. George H. Sabine holds the following view: "The final step in detaching natural law altogether from its entanglement with religious authority was not made by Althusius but by the more philosophically minded Grotius." *A History of Political Theory* (New York: Henry Holt and Company, 1937), p. 420.

2. Natural law and the unwritten law of nations have the same connotation in Grotius. Both are unwritten laws. Van Vollenhoven calls it "the law of mankind," to distinguish it from the written laws arrived at through the agreement of a group of nations. The written laws of the latter kind may be called positive law of nations. *The Framework of Grotius' Book De jure Belli ac Pacis* (1625) (Amsterdam: Ditgave van de N. V. Noord-Hollandsche Uitgeversmaatschappi, 1933), passim. Hereafter referred to as *J.B.P.*

3. Michael B. Foster, *Masters of Political Thought* (New York: Houghton Mifflin Company, 1941), p. 259.

   Sabine's interpretation of Grotius' term "natural law" goes this far, since he says: "For the law of nature would enjoin exactly the same if, by hypothesis, there were no God. Moreover, it cannot be changed by the will of God," op. cit., p. 424.

4. Hugo Grotius, *De Jure Belli ac Pacis Libri Tres, The Classics of International Law*, J.B. Scott, ed. (Oxford: Clarendon Press, 1925), i. I. 10. 56.

5. Clarification between the two usages of the term "natural law" is given by Foster, when Thomas Aquinas is discussed: "His usage of the term 'Natural law' is the opposite of the modern. He confines it to the Eternal law operating in the sphere of rational beings; modern usage confines it to the Eternal law operating in the sphere of irrational nature. Aquinas' Natural law is more like (though not identical with) what in later times was called the Moral law," op. cit., p. 259, n. I.

6. A much better translation here is "natural law."

7. *J.B.P.* i. I. 10. I. Sabine comments on this passage: "The precise meaning of this reference to the command of God is important. In point of fact as Grotius was at pains to make clear, it added nothing in the way of a religious sanction," op. cit., p. 424.

8. *J.B.P.* , ii. 2. 6. 2.

9. The Hegelian principle of the thesis, antithesis, and synthesis is somewhat similar to the mutual relationship among the three parts of the divine law as seen by Grotius. However, the difference between Grotius and Hegel is that the antithesis does not destroy the thesis in order to produce the synthesis. Divine Positive law is, in fact, the second thesis, not the antithesis. It does not destroy the law of nature, but corrects and explains it. The Hegelian principle existed even in Greek philosophy. With Christianity it arrived at its best interpretation. Natural law may be rightly called the proper synthesis.

10. *J.B.P.*, Prolog. 6, 12, 13.

11. Owing to the fact that Natural law is dynamic and the Reason of God is omnipotent and omniscient,

complete human understanding of that law is impossible. To follow God's Will does not mean to know the essence of God.

12. Grotius found himself in a paradoxical situation. Officials of the Catholic church accused him of being a Protestant. The Protestants, on the other hand, often rejected him as a Roman Catholic. Yet, the right judgment is that Grotius was a Catholic in the true sense of the word.

13. *J.B.P.*, Prolog. 48, 50.

14. Ibid., iii, 25. 8.

15. Van Vollenhoven and Sabine share this view.

16. What Aristotle wrote is perfectly true, that certainty is not to be found in moral questions in the same degree as in mathematical science. This comes from the fact that mathematical science completely separates forms from substance, and that the forms themselves are generally such that between two of them there is no intermediate form. *J.B.P.*, ii. 13. I.

17. Ibid., Prolog. 30, 58.

18. "[D]eism is the position that natural theology and rational morality as under stood in the age of reason, are a sufficient content of religion. . . . Orthodox rationalists insisted on both elements of tradition (natural religion and revelation); the radicals, who assumed the name of deists, rejected revelation and reduced religion to these three tenets [the existence of God, the presence of a natural moral law and the certainty of rewards]. . . . The deists went on to attack vigorously all that distinguished Christianity from natural

religion and especially to assail the two supports of revelation, prophecies and miracles. Chubb declared that Jesus himself had been a pure deist." E. D. Dekker, "Deism," *Encyclopedia of the Social Sciences*, ed. E. D. Seligman (New York: Macmillan Co., 1931), V: 61-62.

19. E. D'Entreves, *Natural Law* (London: Hutchinson Library, 1951), 51.

20. *J.B.P.*, i. I. 10. 5.

21. Ibid., Prolog. 11.

22. D'Entreves, in his book *Natural Law*, gives a short but concise exposition of the classical and modern theory of natural law. Op. cit., 70-73.

CHAPTER II:
UNREVEALED DIVINE LAW

That "God created all things" and therefore is the primary source of all law is indisputable for Grotius, but since "God created man . . . with a liberty of acting . . . not in itself evil, but [which] may be the cause of something that is evil,"[1] there appears to be another, secondary, source of law. All laws have their origin in God, but, while Divine laws are created directly by God, human laws are created by man and approved by God. The former ones are eternal; the latter are temporary. The whole system of law may be divided in the following manner: first, Divine law[2] exists outside time — its components, both immanent and transcendent, the law of nature and the Positive Divine law are complementary, and are appointed to apply to all mankind; second, human positive law is limited by time; it consists of the municipal law and of the law of nations. Neither of them is necessarily universal, but both are necessarily dependent on Divine law.

> . . . this whole universe makes but one world, in which there is but one thing that far exceeds the rest in beauty, viz., the sun: and in every man there is but one thing that governs, that is, the mind.[3]

This statement reveals the main characteristics of Grotian thought: there is a perfect Creator of the universe; there is one law in and above all other laws; there is a harmonious unity of the cosmos; and the human mind has access, however imperfect it may be, to the cosmic design of God. Whether writing as a theologian or as a jurist, Grotius follows a well-designed, systematic presentation of the subject matter. For him, God is a perfect "Geometrician" and Supreme Reason, and man, being alike to God, has the potentiality of understanding his own destiny and reconstructing God's design on a smaller scale.

The whole cosmology of Grotius has the underlying presupposition that God is the Lawgiver and the Creator. There is a perfect justice and perfect order in the universe. Man be comes aware of this fact by the power of his reason. By observation of nature, he discovers the existence of the law of nature. Man, however, is not completely bound by this law, since his true allegiance is to Divine law. To this higher law, both the Creator and the creature are committed: God, because Natural law is in the essence of His Being; man, by the fact that he is made in the *imago dei*.

God and the Universe

The harmonious organic universe, as seen by Grotius, cannot exist without a hierarchical arrangement, on both the cosmic and the worldly plane. Thus, God is the highest authority of the whole creation, and man is its most perfect creature, entrusted with the guardianship of the earth. Throughout his works, Grotius discusses the nature of God and of man, and defines religion as a tie between the two. Through it, the relationship between the Creator and his creature is best understood:

> . . . true religion, which is common to all ages, is founded in the main on four principles. The first of these is

that God is and is one; the second, that God is none of the things that are seen, but something more sublime than those; the third, that God has a care for human affairs and judges them with most upright judgments; the fourth, that the same God is the Creator of all things, except himself.[4]

Grotius proves the existence of God using two main arguments: the *prima causa* argument, and the "consent of all nations" argument.

It is clear that things of this world could not have had a beginning in themselves, because everything that exists must have originated from somewhere. In other words, they must have had their beginning in a cause which is the cause of itself. By following the chain of causation, we are bound to arrive at a self-existent cause. This prime cause, the Deity, or God, existing necessarily and not accidentally, is the cause of its own existence and therefore without beginning. To argue that everything that is has its beginning in nothing verges on absurdity, and the only alternative is the sensible answer which leads to the confirmation of the existence of a prime cause from which everything else derives its being.

> . . . our senses show us that some things are made, and things that are made lead us inevitably to something not made.[5]

The notion of the existence of God is innate in man. This notion, a conclusion arrived at by the right use of human reason, has been present in all mankind's history; so, the con sent of the majority of human beings provides another proof for the existence of God. The exceptions to this rule are to be found where men lack real comprehension of the nature of things. Their reasoning stops at the level of the empirical world. Grotius draws a parallel between animals and men. Animals are not aware of the existence of the universe since such awareness requires the capabilities of the human mind.

Men, on the other hand, in addition to understanding their physical environment, have the power to comprehend the reality beyond it, God.

In view of these arguments, the first principle is firmly established: God, the lawgiver and the judge, exists.

The essence of a necessary being consists in its oneness and in its self-existence, qualities which do not allow for the existence of similar beings. Since, in the universe, one thing far exceeds the rest,[6] by analogy there could be only one God, and, therefore, only one original source of law.

God is infinitely perfect. This means that He is living, eternal, of immense power, and infinitely good. In this way, God is different from all other things. It is true that qualities of this kind exist in other things, but, in them, the amount of life, reason, power, and goodness is a matter of degree, while the completeness and perfection of these qualities can be attributed only to God. It must be admitted, therefore, that only laws of God are perfectly good and completely just.

The third principle of religion points to the "governmental" theory of Grotius. According to this theory, the world is governed by the providence of the all-wise and all-powerful God, who possesses infinite knowledge of the present and of the future, and motivates particular things, and especially men, to observe justice and to promote the good of the whole. Every part of the universe, be it the solar system or the most minute organism on the earth, acts under the constant direction of God. The emphatic insistence of Grotius that every action is conditioned by the immanent supervision of God, leaves no place for deistic implications in his thinking. It is a fact that all affairs of the world depend on the Divine Providence. To the same Providence "empires owe their existence," and both men and nature have to comply with it. Grotius also stresses the importance of miracles.[7] This indicates that God participates in human history and that He changes the course of events whenever the necessity arises. The analysis of predictions[8] also confirms the argument that God remains active in the affairs of the world and that he demands adherence to his laws. They witness to the fact that right judgments follow either compliance with or rejection of God's commands.

Finally, as a conclusion of these three principles, the fourth follows inevitably: God is the Creator of all things except Himself. Since God is one, necessary, self-existing Being, without beginning, all other things are created by Him, directly or indirectly. "That the Author of the nature is the most complete understanding . . ."[9] and "that life was infused into things by the Spirit of God"[10] is evident everywhere. The perfect design and the harmony of the universe could have been created only by the Supreme Mind. Grotius gives examples to support the cosmological argument for the existence of God: the heavenly constellations, the motion of the stars and of the planets, the geometrical figure of the earth,[11] and the structure of the human body. All this must be the product of the perfect reason. The work of a Supreme Mind is also exemplified in the pyramidal constitution of created matter: inorganic matter, plants, animals, man. Matter serves as the basis for biological and psychological life. In man, all these elements are intermingled and crowned by his ability to understand the Creator.[12]

God and Mankind

With this central theme of theology clear in his mind, Grotius undertakes an inquiry into the nature of mankind and its relationship to God.

> From these contemplative principles are drawn principles of action, such as that God is to be honored, loved, worshipped and obeyed. . . .[13]
> . . . religion, though it is essentially a means to win the grace of God, has profound effects as well on human society.[14]

"The principles of action" directed to God by man find their full expression when man relates himself to his fellowmen. To do so successfully, he must understand the basic principles of Divine law on which the existence of human society depends: self-love and duty to oneself, love for one's fellow being and the universal concord resulting from the promotion of the welfare of others, universal security through the greatest social virtue justice), and freedom of action and its application through good faith. By these principles, ordained by Natural law and disclosed in the law of nature, men's actions and mutual relationships are guided. Once men take cognizance of them, they can participate in local societies and in the common society of mankind.

> . . . the old poets and philosophers have rightly deduced that love, whose primary force, and action are directed to self-interest, is the first principle of the whole natural order.[15]

The authoritative classical writings that Grotius uses in order to expand this view indicate that the fundamental law of creation directs each individual part of nature to self-preservation, or, in other words, toward realization of its own good. That all things seek their own happiness and security is confirmed by Aristotle, who calls this phenomenon "a manifestation of that true and divinely inspired love which is laudable in every phase of creation."[16] However, immoderate self-interest, the excess of self-love, conflicts with justice and results in vice. The concept of self-love is combined with the concept of duty to oneself. The latter concerns man insofar as good or evil is imposed on him or by him. The imposition of either of these opposites (blessings or ills) has a direct or indirect influence on man's situation:

> among the blessings, life with body whole and healthy, . . . honour, riches, pleasure; . . . among the ills, death,

22

mutilation of the members, disease . . . infamy, poverty, pain.[17]

It follows that man's duty must be the achievement of what is termed good and the suppression of the evil, and, since men live in societies, it is to their own good to promote their common welfare. This is in agreement with the second principle of Natural law, based on the fact that love is twofold: love for oneself and love for others. Such composition of love is found everywhere in nature, but it is most prominently manifested in man, who, being endowed with reason, develops that reason to its greatest degree by following right or universal reason. Right reason, or love in its wider sense, leads to what is meant by the good and the true. When fully employed, it results in universal concord and in the cooperation of nations.

The proper understanding of these two principles of Natural law gives a new insight into Grotian thought. It is indeed difficult to make a clear-cut division between what we have termed Natural law and the law of nature. But here, when the nature of love is discussed, it seems that self-love is the fundamental principle of Natural law. Yet, the two need not be contradictory. When Grotius gives precedence to the love for others over the love for oneself, at the same time he gives precedence to the Natural or Divine law over the law of nature. Thus, he places man not only in created nature, but also above it. That the twofold composition of love is found everywhere in nature, Grotius readily admits,[18] but, according to the law of nature, this is due to instinct and is limited.

In man, the secondary principle of the law of nature (love for others) becomes the primary principle, the self-love is often replaced by, or at least given a new meaning through, love for others. If this line of thought is followed, the statement of Grotius[19] acquires a clear meaning.

The idea of the universal community of mankind has always been in the original design of God and is constantly within the reach of men. The way to its realization requires mutual confidence among men and a full development of the social impulse. This impulse consists of "reciprocal acts and sentiments, and of the intermingling of one's own goods and ills with the goods and ills of others."[20] Finally, the principle of personal justice, derived from duty to oneself, when applied to others, commands the exercise of social justice. Personal freedom entitles man to use his freedom, but the limits to such use are defined by social justice. Since every man is endowed with an equal amount of freedom, the right use of this gift of God demands subjection of individual freedoms to common freedom. Thus, by pursuing the common good, equality is achieved. If, however, the emphasis is put on individual good (the excess of self-love), inequality and the predominance of evil will follow.

Man was created "free and *sui juris*." He remains within his full rights only when he observes these same characteristics in other members of human society. That he will observe freedom and the rights of others can be secured only by "trustworthiness" or by good faith. Good faith is another essential principle of Natural law which supports justice and the social con tract.

Grotius finally draws his conclusion as to what are the duties and the rights of men and of states:

> God wills that we should protect ourselves, retain our hold on the necessities of life, obtain that which is our due, punish transgressors, and at the same time defend the state.[21]

Man acquires his rights from the full observance of his duties. The duties of man, in the first place, are to "honour, love, worship and obey God," since God is the source of justice[22] and "law the unerring mind of God." In the second place, the duty of man is to uphold justice and law. According to Grotius, man's existence is seen in two dimensions: he is subject to natural as well as to moral forces. While for some philosophers of law, justice has its source only in man, for Grotius, law and justice have a moral as well as a legal meaning; for him, God is the source of true justice.

> Law, however, even lacking the support of force is not entirely without influence. For justice brings peace of conscience and injustice torment and anguish, such as Plato describes as inhabiting the breast of tyrants. Good men unite in praising justice and condemning injustice. Most important of all, God is a foe to injustice and though he reserves his judgments for the next life, yet he often makes their power evident in this, as history teaches in manyfold examples.[23]

The conclusion, then, is that Grotius understood the destiny of man to be the promotion of justice and law in, and the achievement of happiness after, this life.[24] In other words, by pursuing these two main objectives, man fulfills his duties. Then, "what Plato and Pythagoreans said, that the end of man is to be made most like to God,"[25] becomes true. The rejection of law and justice is followed by inevitable consequences. The Divine Judge reserved to Himself the final judgment, but, at the same time, He appoints two judges for intervention in human affairs: every act is judged by "conscience, or the innate estimation of oneself, and public opinion, or the estimation of others."[26]

According to Grotius, the ontological origin and source of all law is in God. Men create laws; they are a secondary source of law. But, if these laws are to be just, their true source must always be in God. Grotius separates the two sources only for the sake of making a clear, systematic classification, but, in the final analysis, the reference is always to "the unerring mind of God."

NOTES

1. Hugo Grotius, *De Veritate Religionis Christianae* (*The Truth of Christian Religion*), trans. by John Clarke (Cambridge: J. Hall and Son, 1860), 7, 12. Hereafter referred to as *V.R.C.*

2. Divine and Natural law are used to mean the same thing; this law is in the essence of God's Being.

3. *V.R.C.*, 5.

4. *J.B.P.*, ii. 20. 45. 1. A full, systematic discussion of the above-quoted statement is given in the great apologetic work of Grotius, *The Truth of Christian Religion*, *V.R.C.*, 1-60.

5. Ibid., ii. 20. 45. 3.

6. Supra, 15.

7. "[S]ince God is all-knowing and all-powerful, why should we think him not able to signify his knowledge or his resolution to act, out of the ordinary course of nature, which is hi s appointment, and subject to hi s direction and government?" *V.R. C.*, 16.

8. Numerous examples quoted from the Old Testament and classical writers, ibid., 49.

9. Ibid., 7.

10. Ibid., 28.

11. "The very figure of the world, which is the most perfect, viz., round, and all the parts of it inclosed [sic], as it were in the bosom of the heavens, and placed in wonderful order, sufficiently declare, that these things were not the result of chance, but the appointment of the most excellent understanding." Ibid., 9.

12. In a universal sense, moreover, inferior things were given for use by their superiors. Plants and herbs, for example, were given to the beasts, and beasts — as well as all things in general — to man, inasmuch as man excels in worth all other created things." Grotius uses Genesis 1, Aristotle, and Cicero to confirm this point. Hugo Grotius, *De Jure Praedae Commentarius* (*Commentary on the Law of Prize and Booty*), trans. by Gladys L. Williams (Oxford: Clarendon Press, 1950), 11. Hereafter referred to as *J.Pr.*

13. *J.B.P.*, ii. 20. 45. 3.

14. Ibid., ii. 20. 44. 3.

15. Quotation from Plato Symposium given. *J.Pr.*, 9.

16. Ibid.

17. Ibid., 10.

18. "There are moreover some actions, even of the beasts, so ordered and directed, as plainly discover them to be the effects of some small degree of reason: as is most manifest in ants and bees; . . ." "They "will avoid things hurtfull [sic], and seek those that are profitable to them, . . ." but ". . . are unable to do other things which do not require more pains." Natural reason avoids pain; moral reason can sublimate it. *V.R.C.*, 8.

19. Supra, 5.

20. *J. Pr.*, 14.

21. Ibid., 31.

22. ". . . the very term *ius* (law) is derived from *Iovis* (Jove). . . ." Ibid., 8.

23. *J.B.P.* Prolog. 20.

24. *V.R.C.*, passim.

25. Ibid., 59.

26. Hugo Grotius, *Mare Liberum* (*The Freedom of the Seas*), trans. by R. van Deman Magoffin (New York: (Oxford University Press, 1916), 3. Hereafter referred to as *M.L.*

CHAPTER III:
REVEALED DIVINE LAW

Hugo Grotius felt that natural theology was inadequate for the explanation of Divine laws. Nature and reason did not fully reveal the truth about God. This was made possible through the supernatural revelation of God in Christ. In His Divine Positive law, Christ defined the Will of God.

> Thus what happens is, and how to be secured, men may make some conjectures; but if there be anything concerning it revealed from God, that ought to be esteemed most true and most certain. . . . The design of the second book (after having put up our petitions to Christ the King of heaven, that he would afford us such assistances of His holy spirit, as may render us sufficient for so great a business) is . . . to show that the Christian religion is most true and certain.[1]

Grotius undertook to "show that the Christian religion is most true and certain," and gave one of the strongest apologies for Christianity. For him, Christianity was the final revelation of God to mankind. The Christ event was the turning point of history. Its significance consisted in the fact that God finally fully revealed Himself to the individual, to the nations, and to the whole community of mankind. It should be noted that this revelation was conditioned by the use of faith and reason on the part of man. The character of this religion appealed to both:

> . . . there is nothing in Christian religion either impious or absurd, which any man can pretend against religion recommended by so great miracles, whose precepts are so virtuous, and whose promises are so excellent.[2]

The analysis of the presentation of Christianity given by Grotius indicates a well-ordered system. His discussion follows two main lines of thought. For the first, Grotius used faith; for the second, he employed reason. These were the indispensable and inseparable elements for the understanding of Divine law in its written and unwritten form. On the one hand, faith in divine promises given by Christ had to be complemented by the faith in his miracles, and, above all, by faith in his miraculous resurrection. On the other hand, such faith acquires greater strength when founded on reason. Grotius further argued that right reason could not reject the doctrine of Christ. This doctrine was perfect, since it was propounded by "the most perfect of men."

The Role of Faith

The Divine Positive law provides man with a higher degree of the knowledge of God. At the same time, this insight into the essence of Natural law imposes new obligations upon men. Also, the law of nature is valid only after its redefinition in terms of the new Divine law. The new law takes precedence over the old one, without destroying it. It has to be accepted by faith in the divinity of its lawgiver, who is the exponent of the Will of God. Thus, according to Grotius, the purpose of the law of Christ is to coordinate the expressions of God's

Creativity and of God's Will. So far, man has known God only through His creation. With Christ, this knowledge of God as the Creator was enriched and complemented by the knowledge of God as the Will. Through the combination of the two, men were given the opportunity to adjust their reason to the Reason of God. Therefore, Divine Positive law was the indispensable bridge between the law of nature on one side and Natural law on the other. In other words, in the light of the expressly stated Will of God, men are able to coordinate natural and moral elements in themselves. The precepts of Divine Positive law demand that self-love be rightly used through the love of others. They also demand that individual reason affirm itself through the universal reason. Thus, the completion of this task set before men by Christ is bound to result in greater harmony and unity between God and man, and between man and man.

Grotius stated his strongest belief in the validity of the miracles performed by Christ. He also expressed his faith in Christ's Resurrection. For him, miracles confirmed God's immanence in the world, God's direction of created matter, and God's power to change the law of nature.[3] Since the faith in the doctrine of Christ involved faith in the divine power of the lawgiver to perform miracles a comparison may be drawn between the two laws. The miracles that Christ performed, and the miracle of His Resurrection, contradicted the ordinary current of events in nature. Likewise, His new doctrine asserted the opposite of the human interpretation of the law of nature. Undoubtedly, Grotius stated his position regarding miracles after a thorough examination of this problem. While natural reasoning implied a contradiction, right reason indicated that, in fact, there was no discrepancy involved, since it was in the power of God to change the natural course of events whenever there was a reason for such an action.

Moreover, God neither does nor suffers miracles to be done without a reason; for it does not become a wise lawgiver to depart from his laws without a reason, and that a weighty one. Now no other reason can be given why these things were done, but that which is alleged by Christ, viz., to give credit to his doctrine.[4]

Grotius was not alone in asserting the credibility of miracles. He found support for his belief in theological writings of Christians who, according to him, "were men of good judgment, and of no small learning." For them, as for Grotius, the divine lawgiver was the complete master of nature.

Grotius argued that God was not limited by the laws that He created. It was in His power to restore to life, although, according to the human interpretation of the law of nature, this was impossible. Relying both on his faith and on his reason, Grotius stated:

> Christ's coming to life again in a wonderful manner, after his crucifixion, death, and burial, affords no less strong an argument for those miracles that were done by him. For the Christians of all times and places assert this not only for a truth, but as the principal foundation of their faith: . . . but that a dead man should be restored to life, by the power of him who first gave life to man, there is no reason why this should be thought impossible.[5]

An inquiry into the interpretation of resurrection, as understood by Grotius, is unimportant at this point. It suffices to say that this central event of Christian history was the basis for the faith of Grotius, and that his theological thinking began with it. Whether he understood resurrection symbolically, or as a fact, or as the great mystery, need not be discussed. As a matter of fact, he used various scientific arguments to prove the possibility of resurrection, even according to scientific laws.[6] These arguments were intended to serve the purpose of reconciling the natural reason of man, characterized by the search for factual evidence, with the faith or supernatural reason of man.

The insistence of Grotius on the credibility of miracles is significant. The emphasis on miracles acquires its full meaning when a parallel is drawn between the theological and juridical works of Grotius. Then it becomes clear that the spirit of Grotius the theologian directed the thinking of Grotius the lawyer. Grotius saw that the laws of nature allowed only for the regular course of nature. This law subjected man to the inevitability of death. On the other hand, Grotius' belief in miracles implied the belief in the existence of God and in his intervention in the affairs of men. Miracles, then, were possible according to Divine law. God's power extended over death; therefore, resurrection was possible. The symbolic meaning of the resurrection, transferred to the field of law, suggests the following: first, the precepts of the new Divine Positive law had the power of reshaping the precepts of the old law of nature; second, the "traits of Divine law" were originally put into the hearts of men. Neglected and left to die there, they had to be resurrected by the power of God; third, Christ's coming to life "in a wonderful manner" symbolized for Grotius the constant presence of the new lawgiver in the world. The eternal value of the precepts of the Divine Positive law was bound to change human thought.

Grotius used the ethical precepts of the New Testament to construct his own ethics. He combined this with the moral code of the Old Testament and with the classical theory of the natural law, thus producing a Christian interpretation of law. He expressed the striking importance of Christ's doctrine in the following manner:

. . . Christ himself (as both his own disciples and strangers confess) declared a new doctrine, as by a divine command: it will certainly follow, that this doctrine was true[.][7]

Grotius considered the role of faith for the occurrence of miracles of primary importance. For him, miracles were the result of the action of God in the world, but, at the same time, their occurrence was conditioned by the faith of man. It is certain that Grotius attached the same significance to the role of faith when Christ's divine promises and predictions were in question. Grotius emphasized that both the predictions of Christ regarding His crucifixion, and the promises of God to Christ regarding His resurrection, were fulfilled. God's promises to Christ were kept, because of His unwavering faith. Likewise, the promises of Christ to His disciples and followers are bound to be fulfilled, but only if their faith is unshakable. It must be remembered that faith in Christ and His Law inevitably demands the adjustment of human actions to that law.

Grotius saw the promises and the predictions of Christ fulfilled in two different and yet complementary ways. First, they describe the state of man in the "life after this." Second, the obedience to the law of Christ was also bound to change the situation of man and mankind in the terrestrial dimension.

As regards the God-man relationship, adherence to the Divine law is rewarded with a state in which:

> The mind will have a knowledge of God and of Divine Providence, and whatever is now hidden from it, without any mistake: the will will be calm, employed in wonder and praises, in beholding God; in a word, all things will be much greater and better than can be conceived by comparing them with the greatest and best here.[8]

On the basis of this statement, Grotius may be regarded as a mystic, restating the traditional belief of the Christian church. Christ, says Grotius, disclosed to His disciples the true knowledge of their end by promising another life after this, "in which there should [will] be no more death, pain or sorrow, but [which will be] accompanied with the highest joy." Besides the resurrection of the soul, Christ promised the resurrection of the body, which "will be in a perpetual vigour, and its brightness will exceed the stars."

The rewards for the observance of Divine law were not limited only to the "life after this." On the contrary, the implementation of the principles laid down by Christ is bound to transform man and human society on earth. When men follow these principles, they come to the realization of the common good.[9] The realized common good would inevitably bring about the improvement of the personal good of each separate individual. On a higher level, the states and their rulers would become aware of the fact that the promotion of the good of mankind would bring about the promotion of the good of their individual commonwealths. Grotius believed in the possibility of the realization of Christ's predictions and promises, and ventured to say:

" . . . and [they] shall not lift up sword against nation, neither shall they learn war any more" (Isaiah, II. 4). But this prophesy, as many others, may be taken in a conditional sense. With such an interpretation undoubtedly we are to understand that such will be the state of affairs if all people receive and fulfill the law of Christ; to this end God will not suffer that there be any lack of assistance on His part. It is moreover certain that if all men were Christians, and were living the Christian life, there would be no wars.[10]

It should be noted that the rationalism of Grotius did not impair his realistic considerations concerning human society. He considered wars as an evil imposed by necessity, and discussed the problem of war in order to regulate its conduct. Due to the unstableness of human nature, he thought it unlikely that the community of mankind could achieve perfect unity and harmony. He expected only an approximation to the ideal which Christ set up as the goal.

The Role of Reason

According to Grotius, the most convincing approach to faith must be through reason. Since right reason cannot fail to see the great value of Christianity, it is bound to accept it.

> Another thing in which Christian religion exceeds all other religions that ever were, are or can be imagined, is the exceeding purity and holiness of its precepts, both in those things which concern the worship of God, and also in all other particulars.[11]

Grotius contended that right reason must respond to the revelation of God in Christ. The precepts of the law of Christ confirmed the Divine Positive law given by God to the Hebrews, and the traces of that law found in "the hearts of the wisest of the heathens." For Grotius, then, the perfection of God remained intact, since the successive developments did not mean that Divine law changed in its essence. At the same time, there was no contradiction in God's giving additional commands to man. Quite the contrary was the case: God's dynamism and His constant action in the world demanded from man the fulfillment of new tasks and the adjustment of his actions to the essence of Divine laws. Christ, therefore, appeared as the regulator of this process. His law commanded human action in two spheres: first, true love and the right worship of God; and second, love and respect for one's fellowmen. Fulfillment of these commands leads towards the restoration of man.

As regards the first, the polytheism and religious practices of the heathens were condemned, and the belief in one God as commanded to the Jews was confirmed. But their worship of God as reflected in their religious practices was abolished. As for the second, love and the respect for one's fellowman, as suggested by some of the "heathens,"[12] was now made a command. This same precept, practiced among the Jews but limited only to the members of that nation, with the law of Christ became a rule applicable to all men, irrespective of their national affiliation. The love of the one, true God was commanded to all, and that love was acceptable to God only when transformed into love for all creatures of God.

> . . . the Christian religion teaches us to worship God, who is a most holy Being, with a pure mind, and with such actions, as are in their own nature virtuous, if they had not been commanded.[13]

That the worship of one God resumes its purest form with the commands of Jesus Christ becomes clear after a thorough analysis of the meaning of sacrifice. Grotius compared the vulgar and imperfect interpretation of sacrifice by the heathens, and by the Jews, with the perfect interpretation and example given by Christ.

At this point, full light is thrown upon the differences between the law of nature and the true law of nature. The best exponent of the law of nature, Socrates, advocated self sacrifice for truth. Yet, however noble his sacrifice was, it contained an aristocratic but not a kinetic element. It was incomplete because it aimed only towards the salvation of the individual. It promised "the immortality of the soul." The interpretation of the meaning of sacrifice on the part of the Jews suggested salvation for only one particular nation. With Christ, the meaning of sacrifice reaches its perfection. His selfless sacrifice was the complete kenosis. Its purpose was not only His own salvation. Neither was it for the salvation of only one particular nation. Its purpose was the salvation of mankind as a whole. The sacrifice of Jesus superseded the Socratic and Stoic examples fully exemplified in the Old Testament prophets. Its significance was in the fact that it aimed at "the resurrection not only of the soul but also of the body." In other words, it meant both the transformation of the individual and of the whole body of mankind.

The meaning of sacrifice reflects itself in the practices connected with the worship of God. Grotius discarded the heathen practices in accordance with the law of nature. For him, animal and human sacrifices indicated a complete departure from and a contradiction of the true law of nature. On the other hand, Jewish practices were not a part of the Divine law. They were the invention of men.[14] Even if these sacrifices were demanded earlier, Christ abolished them, because the emphasis on rites and ceremonies tended to overshadow the central commands of God. Jesus demanded the return to the essentials of the covenant. He reaffirmed the commandments of the Divine law given to the Hebrews. Grotius found these precepts in the Old Testament: "*To offer sacrifices is not acceptable to thee, neither art thou delighted with burnt offerings: But the sacrifice which thou truly delights in is a mind humbled by the sense of its faults; for thou, O God, will not despise a broken and contrite heart*" (Psalm 60). God really demanded two things: First, "*that which I earnestly commanded them was, that they should be obedient to me;*" (Jeremiah 7) . . . *And that they should walk in the way that I should teach them. So should all things succeed prosperously to them.*" Second, "*Loving kindness towards men is much more acceptable to me than sacrifice; to think aright of God is above all burnt offerings*" (Hosea 7). Grotius found the commands of God well defined in the prophet Micah: "*that you render to every man his due, that you do good to others, and that you become humble and lowly before God.*"

This basic part of Divine law was confirmed by Christ. Its nonessential parts were redefined and given the full meaning:

> Thus it [Christian religion] does not bid us to circumcise our flesh, but our desires and affections: not to abstain from all sorts of works, but only from all such as are unlawful: not to offer the blood and fat of beasts in sacrifice to God; but if there be a just occasion, to offer our own blood for a testimony of the

truth: and whatever share of our goods we give to the poor, we are to look upon as given to God.[15]

Endowed with divine power, Jesus Christ abolished heathen and Jewish sacrifices and offerings. He redirected the minds of men from nature to God. Jesus is thus seen by Grotius as the culmination of human reason. The reason of Christ was at one with the reason of God. It commanded love and obedience to God, and love and unselfish service to one's neighbor. Grotius draws his conclusion from the study of the New Testament:

> But the chief part of religion is everywhere declared to consist in such a godly faith, by which we may be framed to such a sincere obedience, as to trust wholly upon God, and have a firm belief of his promises; whence arises hope, and a true love, both of God and of our neighbour, which causes obedience to his commands.[16]

The role of Christ consisted in the reestablishment of the broken ties between God and man. Such restoration of man was to be effected through the obedience of man to Divine law and to the divine lawgiver, who stated the essence of His commands in a concise manner:

> The sum of it [Christian religion] is wonderful for its substantial brevity: that we should love God above all things, and our neighbour as ourselves; that is we should do to others as we would have them do to us.[17] Hence, the purpose of Divine Positive law. was twofold: first, this law demanded a new understanding of religion; second, it provided the basis for the new ethics. For instance: concerning modesty, temperance, goodness, moral virtue, prudence, the duty of governors, and subjects, parents and children, masters and servants, husbands and wives; and particularly,

abstaining from those vices, which under a show of virtue deceived many of the Greeks and Romans, *viz.*, the desire of honour and glory.[18]

Grotius insisted on the dynamic character of the immanence of God. Due to this fact, God's action in the world could be perceived in two ways: in His enactment of the new laws, and in His abrogation of the incorrect interpretation of Divine laws on the part of man. As regards the first, it has been shown that the dynamism of Divine Positive law demands the new approach to religion. Likewise, that same law commands the adjustment of man's actions to the new moral code. In religion, the love of God is to be complemented by the love for all human beings. Such love does not impair self-love, but gives it its full meaning. In the field of morals, Divine Positive law reaffirms the principles of the classical ethics of the Greeks and of the Romans. It demands the practice of the virtues of humility, patience, and charity without destroying the virtues of temperance, fortitude, and discretion. As for the second, Grotius saw the dynamism of the Divine Positive law in its corrective role. The religious practices of human and animal sacrifice were condemned. The "moral" precepts of honor and glory were rejected.

It may be concluded from reading Grotius that Divine Positive law did not destroy the true law of nature. However, this law removed the false and imperfect rendering of its precepts by men. For the Reason of God, Divine Positive law was the dynamic evolution of the unchangeable, but not static, true law of nature. According to it, God had the power to enact the Resurrection. It was in the power of God to command the new precepts of ethics. For the reason of man, Divine Positive law was a revolution contradicting the human understanding of the law of nature. The Resurrection was a revolution for the ordinary course of events in nature. At the same time, the new ethics was a negation of the ethics established by men.

It is now clear where Grotius saw the difference between the law of nature and the Divine Positive law, or, to put it in another way, the distinction between Natural law as partly understood by the wisest of heathens and Natural law as fully revealed by Jesus Christ. The approach to the first was through natural reason; the approach to the second, through moral reason, which implied faith, love, and hope.

The Role of History

For his approach to Christianity, Grotius used faith and reason. These two elements had to be supported by the element of historical evidence. According to Grotius, the historicity of Jesus of Nazareth could not be doubted or denied, since historical records confirmed the fact of His existence. With the insight of a historian, Grotius quoted historical writings of both the followers and the enemies of Christianity. These records, taken from both sides, testified that Jesus lived, was crucified, and was worshipped after His death. These same sources discussed the human personality of the new lawgiver.

Grotius concluded that the final form of Divine Positive law was given to men through a person who, in his human life, stood above all other human beings. Because of His purity and perfection, Jesus was the man and the teacher. The author of Christian doctrine far exceeded the authors of either Stoicism or Judaism.[19] His code of ethics was not separated from His person. In other words, Grotius suggests that a perfect law was given by a perfect lawgiver, who practiced whatever He taught.

[Christ], as described by his disciples to be without any manner of sin . . . performed himself what he commanded . . . he was the most patient of injuries and torments, as is evident from his punishment on the cross; he was so great a lover of mankind, of his enemies, even of those by whom he was led to death, that he prayed to God for them.[20]

Thus, for Grotius the historian, the perfection of Christ's human life and the integrity of His personality pointed to the divinity of the law He gave to men.

Divine Positive law belongs to what Grotius called "volitional divine law." The law of Christ gave the perfect form of God's Will.

This law, moreover, was given either to the human race, or to a single people. To the human race we find that the law was thrice given by God: immediately after the creation of man, a second time in the renewal of human kind after the Flood, lastly in the more exalted renewal through Christ.

These three bodies of divine law are beyond doubt binding upon all men, so far as they have be come adequately known to man.[21]

The purpose of volitional divine law was to direct the actions of men. It differed from the law of nature proper, since the former originated in God's Will and the latter in God's Creativity. Volitional divine law given on two occasions to man remains outside recorded historical facts. Here, Grotius repeats the biblical narrative. Man's ability to understand this law was not completely impaired by man's departure from God. In fact, the human definition of this law may be placed in the context of mankind's history. Thus, the "wisest of heathens," and the most righteous "among the Hebrews," arrived independently at a knowledge of God's will by observing nature in and around themselves. Even more, according to Grotius, the Hebrew nation was helped directly by God, who gave them His expressed commands.

In other words, Grotius is saying that both the classical Greek and the Old Testament traditions simultaneously, but independently, arrived at the theory of natural law.

However, in both cases, and due to imperfect human interpretation, this theory reached a stalemate. The agnosticism of the Greek tradition brought natural law theory to the level of the law of nature, thus limiting the transcendental potentiality of man's reason. The nationalism of the Jewish tradition arrested the spreading of Divine law to other nations, thus limiting the knowledge of the law of mankind only to one particular nation.

For Grotius, the third occasion on which God gave his law to mankind occurred in history. The law of Christ, ontological in its character, bestowed new dynamism upon the almost static, epistemological norms of natural law theory found in the Greek and in the Jewish tradition. The law of Christ was intended to revolutionize human thought and to redirect human actions. In addition to the human interpretation of God's will, Christ gave the Divine interpretation of that will, thus indicating, first, the transcendental character of human reason, and second, the universal application of the law of mankind.

Grotius presents two interpretations of the law of mankind: first, the human reading of that law in nature; second, Christ's definition of that law as derived from Divine law. The function of the law of Christ is, therefore, to lead man from the first to the second stage.

Thus, two systems of ethics may be discerned in Grotius. The comparison of the two systems implies the contrast of the two, the higher value of the law of mankind as defined by Christ, and the demand on men to use their potential abilities for implementing the precepts of Christian ethics.

NOTES

1. *V.R.C.*, 59, 60.

2. Ibid., 180.

3. The phrase "law of nature" here does not involve the essence of God.

4. *V.R.C.*, 64.

5. Ibid., 65, 68.

6. Ibid., 65ff.

7. Ibid., 69.

8. Ibid., 72.

9. The common as well as the individual good refers to the peace of mind, just as it refers to the material peace.

10. *J.B.P.*, i. 2. 8. I.

11. *V.R.C.*, 75.

12. Stoics, Plato, Aristotle, Cicero, etc., are repeatedly quoted in *V.R.C.* and other works.

13. *V.R.C.*, 76.

14. "Thus much is evident certainly, that the Hebrews were desirous of very many rituals; which was a

sufficient reason why God should enjoin them such a number, upon this account, lest the memory of their dwelling in Egypt should cause them to return to the worship of false Gods." Ibid., 152.

15. Ibid., 77.

16. Ibid., 80. This compendium of Grotius is the summing up of several passages from the New Testament.

17. Ibid., 85.

18. Grotius enumerates places in the New Testament where each particular problem is discussed. Here, in fact, he presented a condensation of the traditional Christian ethics. He developed these precepts in his legal works. Ibid., 85.

19. "The authors of the Grecian wisdom and knowledge themselves confessed, that they alleged scarce any thing for certainty, . . . and the mind as dim-sighted in regard to divine things. . . . Beside there was hardly any of them, but was addicted to some particular vice: . . . Moses, the Hebrew lawgiver, was an excellent person, however not entirely free from faults." Ibid., 87-88.

20. Ibid., 88-89.

21. *J.B.P.* i. I. 15. 1.

Cover, *Syntagma Arataeorum* (Grotius' version of Solensis Aratus'
Phaenomena). Leiden, 1600

Portrait of Hugo Grotius aged 15, half-length, holding a medallion
with Henri IV on a chain, in an oval. 1599

46

HUGONIS GROTII

De

JURE PRAEDAE

COMMENTARIUS.

Ex Auctoris Codice descripsit et vulgavit

H. G. HAMAKER, etc.

HAGAE COMITUM

APUD MARTINUM NIJHOFF.

CIƆIƆCCCLXVIII.

AN UNPUBLISHED WORK OF HUGO GROTIUS'S

TRANSLATED FROM AN ESSAY
IN DUTCH (1868) WRITTEN BY THE LATE

ROBERT FRUIN
Professor of National History in the University of Leyden

De Jure Praedae Cover, 1604

47

Annotated Manuscript Page, *De Jure Praedae*, 1604

Grotius Age 25, 1608

Artist Michiel Jansz. van Mierevelt

De Jure Belli ac Pacis, 1625, 1670

Dutch War and Politics 1618

De Veritate Religionis Christianae, 1622

Introduction to Roman-Dutch Law, 1631

Mare Liberum, 1633

Grotius, 1636

THE ILLUSTRIOUS
HUGO GROTIUS
OF THE LAW OF
WARRE
AND
PEACE
WITH
ANNOTATIONS.
III. *PARTS.*
AND
Memorials of the Author's
Life and Death.

Translated by *C. B.* Master of Arts.

'Ο ἀδικῶν ἀσεβεῖ M. Antonin. Imp. l. 9.

LONDON,
Printed by *T. Warren*, for *William Lee*, And are to be
sold at his shop, at the signe of the *Turki-head*
in *Fleet-street*, M. DC. LV.

Law of Warre and Peace, 1655

55

Law of Warre and Peace, 1707

HVGO GROTIVS,
Reginæ Regnique Suedici Consiliarius, eorundemque ad
Regem Christianissimum Legatus ordinarius. quondam
Syndicus Roterodamensis, ejusdemque Urbis in Conventu
Ordinum Hollandiæ & Westfrisiæ Delegatus.

Grotius, 1670

SAMUELIS PUFENDORFII

DE

JURE NATURÆ
ET GENTIUM
LIBRI OCTO.

Cum Gratia & Privilegio S. Regiæ Majestatis Sueciæ.

LONDINI SCANORUM

Sumtibus ADAMI Junghans imprimebat

VITUS Haberegger / *Acad. Typogr.*

ANNO M DC LXXII.

Samuelis Pufendorfij, *De Jure Naturae et Gentium*
Libri Octo, 1672

Grotius, 1727

CHAPTER IV:
THE LAW OF MANKIND AND PEACE

The preceding inquiry into the works of Grotius, covering his study of the nature of God, man, and human society, allows for the following conclusions: first, the problem of the existence of man and the problem of the destiny of man can be stated in three different ways. Man is viewed: as an atomized unit existing independently of other members of the human race, as a unit related to other human beings, and as a unit related to God. While Grotius does not consider the first proposition as a solution, his second and his third propositions are closely linked, and they offer the solution to man's predicament. Thus, according to Grotius, the proper relationship of man and God is bound to produce a positive relationship between man and man.

The second deduction from the works of Grotius refers to the freedom of man. The actions of man are in accordance with three potential, and, at the same time, successive, levels:[1] first, the level of nature, on which man is determined to the greatest degree, and on which man's actions follow the principles of the law of nature; second, the level of human reason, on which moral actions result from the restraints of human natural instincts and impulses — principles of natural law are applicable here; finally, the third level, on which man can act contrary to nature and in accordance with the principles of Divine Positive law. The degree of the freedom of action depends on the degree to which man has developed his potentialities.[2] The nature of man's freedom is such that by using it he can enter into the dynamic process of his positive growth. In this case, man can create a situation of peace and justice, and, thus, cooperate with the divine dynamism.

Third, divine laws apply equally to man and to mankind. The law of nature provides for the preservation of the individual. Natural law provides for the preservation of the commonwealth of mankind. Divine Positive law leads toward a balance between the two, directing man to the proper understanding of self-love and of the love for others. This law is the expression of God's Will and may be rightly called the law of mankind. The analysis of law, therefore, has to be approached from one main aspect: "*What God has shown to be his will that is law.*"[3]

Fourth, man and society have a teleological purpose. In other words, the Will of God becomes the *telos* of human existence. The will of man and the will of the state are dynamically directed toward approximate unity with the Will of God. Human laws are, therefore, formulated to bring about this unity. Human laws are the necessary cohesive force for human associations. According to Grotius, these laws are the product of the will of man, but their validity depends on their compatibility with the Will of God.

> Human law, then, is either municipal law, or broader in scope than municipal law, or more restricted than municipal law. Municipal law is that which emanates from civil power. The civil power is that which sways over the state. The state is a complete association of free men, joined together for the enjoyment of rights and for their common interest. The law which is narrower in scope than municipal law, and does not come from the civil power, although subject to it, is

of varied character. It comprises the commands of a father. . . . The law which is broader in scope than municipal law is the law of nations; that is the law which has received its obligatory force from the will of all nations, or of many nations.[4]

By constructing an overall scheme of the law, it becomes clear how Grotius related different branches of the law binding on human associations. Their mutual relationship is better understood once their individual relationship to the law of mankind is apprehended. Since Grotius insisted that human will derives its power from the divine Will, human laws fit into the law of mankind only if the will of man follows the lead of the Will of God.

God's Will appointed the smallest and the largest community of man, namely, the family and mankind. Man's will established other communities, covering the area between the family and the society of all men. To this area, belong the laws of townships and of municipalities, of chartered companies, and of other private bodies. Human will also created the laws of states and laws binding on the limited-state groups. These groups, either alliances or confederacies, are the intermediate associations between the separate states and the society of mankind. Peace and justice will be preserved if the law of mankind is observed on all levels: man to man, man to the state, state to the society of mankind.

Precepts of the Law of Nature

All arguments of Grotius rest on two main propositions: first, the Will and the design of God; and second, the common consent of mankind. The second rule of "Dogmatica" reads: *What the common consent of mankind has shown to be the will of all, that is law.* Grotius concludes that right reason must inevitably coincide with the reason of God and with universal reason. Starting from this point, he confirms Cicero's view of the nature of human society:

> Just as all bodily members function in mutual harmony because it is to the advantage of the whole that the individual parts be preserved, even so mankind will show forbearance toward individuals because we are born for a life of fellowship. Society, too, can be kept safe from harm only by love and watchful care of its component parts.[5]

This natural association of all men was appointed by God. Its origin is found in the basic human association, also appointed by God, in which "the divine law unites the two in marriage."

> The most natural association appears in marriage. . . . Christ did not establish a new law, but restored the law which God the Father had established in the beginning.[6]

Thus, Grotius saw the constant presence of God in the world reflected in God's constant care for the preservation of the individual family, and in the preservation of its counterpart, the family of mankind. God's original design for mankind indicates that, at first, all things were given to men in common. However, with the multiplication of mankind and with the development of arts and industry, the need for private property appeared. Thus, the original law as regards property was readjusted by the introduction of private property. At the same time, a large number of things given to men still had to be enjoyed in common. The equal right of all men to common ownership strengthened the ties of mankind. Divine justice demanded that nations supply the needs of one another and that they regard the products of one region as the products native to all nations. It was obvious that this was the design of God, since the system of exchange was workable. The oceans and the winds were given free. The access of one nation to the other was unimpaired by nature. The freedom of commerce was a right common to all. The sharing of this right equaled the sharing of the air and of the sun by all.

Universal reason indicated that, for the maintenance of the fellowship among men, certain things had to remain in common. Likewise, the same reason approved the introduction of private property. This new rule became a part of the law of nature, and it became necessary to protect private ownership in the same way as life was protected. Thus, Grotius postulated the two main precepts of the law of nature concerning individuals: first, *It shall be permissible to defend (one's own) life and to shun that which threatens to be injurious*; second, *It shall be permissible to acquire for oneself and to retain, those things which are useful for life*. These two precepts are in accordance with the instincts inborn in man, namely, with the instincts of self-preservation, of self-love, and of the possession of property. It may be concluded that human instincts lead men to what is termed good in a narrow sense.

According to Grotius, the law of Christ helped to establish the just limits showing the extent to which the pursuit of one's own good can go. In other words, this law explained the term "good" in its complete form: "the true love of self regarded as the *prototypon* or prototype, found its fulfillment in the *ektypos* or the image, which is the love for others."

> . . . in accordance with a well-ordered love, the good of an innocent person should receive consideration before the good of one who is guilty, and the public good before that of the individual.[7]

The broadened self-love imposed duties on each individual: *Let no one inflict injury upon his fellow; let no one seize the possession of another, and, Good deeds must be recompensed;*

evil deeds must be corrected. These precepts demanded the defense of the innocent and the punishment of the wicked. Their observance was the foundation for every society. They implied the "social justice" equally accessible to all members of the society. Here, again, Grotius found that Christ's law, properly interpreting the law of nature, gave precedence to the common good. For its preservation, evil has to be punished. With this view in mind, the meaning of the passage found in Matthew becomes clear:

> "Ye have heard that it hath been said, an eye for an eye and a tooth for a tooth; but I say unto you, Resist not him that is evil" (in Hebrew, "the wicked man," which the Greeks translate "him that doeth a wrong"). . . . "but whosoever shall smite thee on thy right cheek, turn to him the other also."[8]

Christ, in fact, demanded that the execution of "social justice" be performed by the persons appointed through the united will of all members of the society. The law of nature allowed for the direct execution of punishment, but the established Jewish law, being the expression of an ordered society, demanded that the "evildoers" be judged by the magistrates.

Finally, the law of nature commands that the exercise of natural liberty be allowed to everyone. To this effect, the last precept of the law of nature, *What each individual has indicated to be his will, that is law with respect to him*, regulated the coordination of many individual wills in a society. The observance of this precept meant the exercise of good faith. Through this medium, God has made it possible that every individual pursue his own good without infringing on the good of others. Good faith provided assurance for the individual members of society. It kept natural liberty intact, and, at the same time, prevented the infringement upon someone else's liberty.

The three rules, combined with the six main precepts of the law of nature, served as the foundation out of which sprang the precepts of the municipal law and the written law of nations. These basic principles remained valid all throughout, and they made possible the exercise of the two great rights of man: freedom of action and the possession of property. Through cultivating liberty and ownership, other appointments of God developed, namely, the multiplication of mankind, the exchange of goods, commerce, and, finally, the formation of commonwealths. When the human race became very large, the law of nature proved insufficient for the maintenance of mankind, and man appeared as the secondary lawgiver. The new laws were based on the principles of the law of nature, but derived their origin from the will of man. It must be noted here that, in spite of the appearance of human positive laws, man remained basically free from these laws, in the sense that men could always turn back to the original rule: What God has shown to be His Will, that is law. Grotius justified such action by stating the last rule of his "Dogmatica": *In cases where (the laws) can be observed simultaneously, let them all be observed; where this is impossible, the law of superior rank shall prevail.* In all instances, for Grotius, God's laws were superior to the human laws.

> Among all good men one principle at any rate is established beyond controversy, that if the authorities issue any order that is contrary to the law of nature or to the commandments of God, the order should not be carried out. For when the Apostles said that obedience should be rendered to God rather than men, they appealed to an infallible rule of action, which is written in the hearts of all men.[9]

Precepts of Human Law and the State

The common human society which originally existed and in which the service to the common good was performed directly by individuals was reshaped by the formation of many commonwealths. Human laws created associations "in which many fathers of families unite into a single people and state." Men, according to Grotius, created the state through their own consent and social contract. This system of organization, a product of human will, was then sanctioned by God.

> This system of organization (commonwealth — *res publica*) has its origin in God the King, who rules the whole universe and to whom, indeed (so the philosophers declare) nothing achieved on earth is more acceptable than those associations and assemblies of men which are known as states (*civitates*).[10]

God approved the associations and assemblies of men described as states, because they fulfilled His purpose. By organizing into the individual societies, by coordinating their work and exchange of goods, men could achieve greater prosperity. In order to maintain a commonwealth, the citizens entered a civil covenant. Only through obedience to the civil covenant could citizens maintain the state, this "condensed version of the universal society."

Obedience implied adherence to God's Will, coupled with respect for the will, natural equity, and the good faith of all. Once established, the precepts of the law of nature expressed by human will[11] were expanded and formulated as *lex* (statutory law).[12]

> This law proceeds from God . . . It is approved by the common consent of all mankind . . . the mutual agreement and the will of individuals. . . . "the common pact of the state."[13]

On the basis of the system thus far developed, another rule was arrived at, namely, *Whatever the commonwealth has indicated to be its will, that is law (ius) in regard to the whole body of citizens.* In this way, the citizens acquired the power to pronounce judgments, valid for their own commonwealths. The prime purpose of the *jus* was to foster equality, concord, and public tranquility. Christ confirmed the validity of civil authority and civil laws as long as they complied with justice and peace. Even more, He commended His disciples to obey all civil laws.

> In the New Covenant Christ enjoined men "to render unto Caesar the things that are Caesars." By this He meant that his followers owed to sovereign powers an obedience joined, if need be, with long suffering, not less in degree, if not even greater, than that which the Jews owed to the Jewish kings.[14]

Grotius contended that the advocacy of the obedience to civil laws as found in the Scriptures, and especially in St. Paul, came about for two main reasons: first, citizens should obey public authorities and look upon them as if they had been established by God himself; second, the constituted order con tributes to the individual as well as to the common good.

Simultaneously with the setting up of the judicial system in a state, the citizens accepted that *Whatever the commonwealth has indicated to be its will, that is law for the individual citizens in their mutual relations.* In other words, the will of the commonwealth now had the power to pass judgments applicable to individual cases. Settlement of disagreements between individuals became the right of the commonwealth. *No citizen shall seek to enforce his own right against a fellow citizen, save by judicial procedure.*

Archons, or *magistrates*, were appointed for the administration of civil affairs. To perform these duties, the *magistratus*, that is to say, any sovereign ruler, had legislative, judicial, and executive powers.[15] Men have associated in states by exercising the power of free will. Through the same medium of the free will they have delegated the execution of justice to their sovereigns; and, according to Grotius, God confirmed this arrangement. "Such is the purport of the saying, 'Kings are from Jove.'"

The Book of Ecclesiastes is witness to the same fact:

> From this same source the force of civil laws is derived as is the power of judgment, given from above by Jesus Himself, the Author thereof. Thus Divine Wisdom of which all human wisdom is but "a fragment," or offshoot, as it were, is represented as saying: "Councel [sic] is mine, and sound wisdom: I am understanding; I have strength. By men kings reign, and princes decree justice. By me princes rule, and nobles, even all the judges of the earth."[16]

The contract of the magisterial mandate between the prince and the citizens imposed duties on both parties: first, *the magistrate shall act in all matters for the good of the state;* second, *the state shall uphold as valid every act of the magistrate.* In accordance with the view that magistrates receive their right of action from God once the consent of the people has been granted, and in order to confirm their authority as legislators and as judges, Grotius introduced the following precepts: *What the magistrate has indicated to be his will, that is law in regard to the whole body of citizens; What the magistrate has indicated to be his will, that is law in regard to the citizens as a whole.*

Grotius found that the Sacred Scriptures confirmed the establishment and maintenance of the state. Even more, they pointed to the source of the power of the rulers:

> Even what could be clearer than the exhortation of Paul? "Let every soul be subject to higher powers. For there is no power but of God. The powers that are ordained by God; and they that resist shall receive to themselves damnation. For rulers are not a terror to good works, but to the evil."[17]

While in agreement with the Christian emphasis on obedience to the rulers and nonresistance to their laws, Grotius indicated that the Divine Positive law allowed resistance in cases of dire necessity:

> More serious is the question whether the law of nonresistance should bind us in case of extreme and imminent peril. Even some laws of God, although stated in general terms, carry a tacit exception in case of extreme necessity. . . . "Danger to life breaks the Sabbath."
> This exception was approved by Christ, as also an exception in the case of another law, which forbade the eating of shewbread.[18]

Drawing an analogy, Grotius suggests that the resistance to the human law is also allowed, especially when the rulers establish laws that contradict the law of mankind. Subjects, therefore, have the right to disobey such laws, and they are encouraged to terminate the rule of a sovereign who is a tyrant. Grotius finds the support for this argument in Thomas Aquinas. "The Angelic Doctor" says that the rule of a tyrant is unjust, because "it is directed to private advantage instead of to the public good." It is wrong to charge with sedition per sons who instigate rebellion against the regime of such a ruler. The charge of sedition more readily applies to the tyrant who encourages discord and civil dissention in order to rule in greater security. To overthrow his rule and to establish law and justice, and thus secure peace and order, is in accordance with the law of mankind.

Precepts of the Law of Nations

The structure of law thus far erected by Grotius indicates that the unwritten law of mankind served for the construction of laws binding men's associations. The state laws appear as the final authority in human legislation. The same law of mankind provided for rules and regulations necessary for the coordination of all states in the commonwealth of mankind. In the first case, the law of nature and its written corollary, the *lex*, regulated relationships between individuals; the state guaranteed the rights and determined the duties of citizens. In the second case, the law of nations regulated relationships of states, pointing to their rights and duties. This law barely existed in a written form. In discussing the law of mankind binding on all commonwealths, Grotius spoke about the primary and the secondary law of nations.

The primary law of nations commands the superiority of the common good over the individual good. In other words, the common good of mankind as a whole is above the common good of the individual states. The confirmation of this law, rightly called the law of mankind, comes from the consensus of all nations. The secondary law of nations is a mixture of the primary law of nations and the statutory laws of individual states. While the primary law of nations is unwritten, the secondary law of nations usually takes the positive form.

> . . . owing to the existence of a common good of an international nature, the various peoples who had established states for themselves entered into agreements concerning that international good.[19]

The agreements between states were possible through the exercise of the free will of each individual state. The state personified in its ruler agrees to coordinate its will with the will of another state. This was made possible since, by the consent of all individuals in a commonwealth, the principle of *sui juris* has been transferred from the individual to the state, each state acquired its own will. In order to avoid differences, and in order to coordinate the multiplicity of the particular laws of different states, all states have to observe the following rule of the law of mankind: *Whatever all states have indicated to be their will, that is law in regard to all of them.* To exemplify this point, Grotius enumerated only "the inviolability of ambassadors, the right of sepulchre, and other institutions of similar kind."[20] Such institutions, whether pacts or customs, have the force of contracts which cannot be dissolved without judicial procedure. Neither the state nor any citizen thereof shall seek to enforce his own right against another state or its citizen, save by judicial procedure.

The question of judicial procedure as concerning states presents the difference between the statutory law of the individual states and the positive law of nations. At the same time, it presents the problem of the judicial authority of one state over the other.[21] While the citizens, in disputes with one another or with the state, are subject to the state, one state is not in subjection but in contraposition to another state.

> Truly, there is no greater sovereign power set over the power of the state and superior to it, since the state is a self-sufficient aggregation.[22]

The following rule should, therefore, be applied in cases of conflict between states: *In regard to judicial procedure, precedence should be given to the state which is the defendant; but if the said state proves remiss in the discharge of its judicial duty, then that state shall be the judge, which is itself the plaintiff.* The state which is the aggressor transgresses the law of nations. Grotius now draws an analogy between the law of nature and the law of nations. According to the former, each individual has the right to be his own judge; according to the latter, each state has the same right. Both laws, as long as they are in accordance with the law of mankind, permit resort to force and waging a just war against the aggressor.

For the purpose of self-preservation, man, following the law of nature and using his will, creates the state. The state, its law, and its ruler thus become the final authority, allowing for no other authority or any other human positive law. In such a situation, and in case God is removed from the affairs of men, coordinating these "self-sufficient aggregations" becomes difficult. At this point, Grotius offers his solution, namely, the Sovereignty of God, whose power is above all in moral force.[23] The law of mankind, or the unwritten law of nations, now resumes its full significance.

Grotius suggested that the Holy Writ should serve as the basis for settling controversies between nations. In this way, peace, freedom, and equity, all the result of justice, will be preserved.

> Considerably better and more dependable is the method chosen by those who prefer to have such questions decided on the basis of the Holy Writ, except that the persons employing such method frequently cite simple historical accounts or the civil law of the Hebrews, in the place of divine law.[24]

For Grotius, compliance with the Divine Positive law secures peace and justice in the family of nations. The same law should serve as the guide for breaking any deadlocks in international affairs. Divine Positive law is in fact the law of mankind stated in its positive terms.

The practical application of this law Grotius entrusts to Christian princes. According to him, Christian princes, being endowed with both faith and reason, should undertake the task of preserving the peace and preventing wars.

> Especially, however, Christian kings and states are bound to pursue this method of avoiding wars. . . . Both for this and for other reasons it would be advantageous, to hold certain conferences of Christian powers, where those who have no interest at stake may settle the disputes of others, and where, in fact, steps, may be taken to compel parties to accept peace on fair terms.[25]

In the second place, Grotius suggested the creation of alliances leagues, and confederations. The best association of this type was, for Grotius, the community of all Christian states. He considered such an alliance as the society of mankind on a small scale.

> . . . since all Christians are members of one body, and are bidden to share one another's sufferings and misfortunes, just as this principle applies to individuals, so also it is applicable to peoples as such, and to kings as such. For every man ought to serve Christ not only personally, but also with the power that has been entrusted to him.[26]

In the third place, although Grotius regarded national and racial ties as strong, for him, "the common bond of human nature" was above any other tie. He considered that, for the defense of justice, alliances between Christians and non-Christians should be made, even if the punishment is to go to another Christian nation that disregarded justice.

> Moreover, the law of the Gospel made no change in this matter. Rather it extends even greater favour to treaties by which those who are strangers to the true religion receive help in a just cause; for the doing of good to all men, whenever there is opportunity, has not only been left free and praiseworthy, but has even been enjoined by precept.[27]

The law of Christ gave the proper interpretation of the term "neighbours."[28] This term applies to every human being. That the protection of the infidels from injury is never unjust was confirmed by the famous parable of the Good Samaritan. Therefore, Grotius concludes: Divine Positive law indicates that the general law of mankind applies to all nations and to all men.

God appointed justice through which the society of mankind is held together. For Grotius, the purpose of justice is the cultivation of the good. In every society, just as in nature, there is good, which is reduced to unity, identity, and equality. Hence, the task of justice is to promote these elements in the society of mankind. God and man have to cooperate in this field. God gave to men the feeling of mutual regard, so that man should love and protect man. Grotius' main argument was that the maintenance of justice is bound to preserve peace. He says that many theologians contended that peace and justice "differ not in fact but merely in name." Peace is the fruit of justice.

Grotius emphasized the role of religion in the society of mankind. Since religion brings man nearer to God, it also points man to the true source of justice.

> Religion is of even greater use in that greater society than in that of a single state. For in the latter the place of religion is taken by the laws and the execution of the laws; while on the contrary in that larger community the enforcement of law is very difficult, seeing that it can only be carried out by armed force, and the laws are very few. Besides, these laws themselves receive their validity chiefly from fear of the divine power; and for this reason those who sin against the law of nations are everywhere said to transgress divine law.[29]

Grotius did not propose a new universal religion. For him, Christianity was sufficient to provide the necessary rules of the law of mankind and to maintain the peace in the family of nations. Grotius says that "the Lord has bestowed His peace" on Christians. Hence, they must endeavor to seek peace with all men, and condone offenses, damages and expenses as long as it is possible to have peace with sufficient safety.

Grotius found that the principle of good faith plays an important role for the maintenance of both peace and justice. According to Cicero, good faith is the foundation of justice, and, according to Simonides, justice is not only giving back what one has received, but also the speaking of truth. Therefore, Grotius argues, good faith is indispensable for human society and must be observed in all actions of men. If good faith is removed from the society of mankind, "all intercourse among men will cease to exist."

Good faith is one of the basic principles of the law of mankind, from which promises, contracts, and oaths derive their origin. They are essential in man-to-man relationships. The insistence of Grotius on the importance of keeping promises which one man gives to another man coincides with his emphasis on the promises which God gave to man.

> . . . God Himself, who cannot be bound by any established law, would act contrary to His nature if He did not make good His promises. . . . From this it follows that the obligation to perform promises arises from the nature of immutable justice, which in its own fashion is common to God and to all beings possessed of reason.[30]

Contracts must also be based on the principle of good faith. In every contract, Grotius demanded equality and fair dealing. He applied this rule to all human beings, irrespective of their creed, race, or nation. Grotius then proceeded to discuss oaths, which must be based on good faith. They are used to confirm promises, agreements, and contracts. Here, the law of Christ made a change, since it demanded that, except in extreme cases, Christians should abstain from oaths.

Promises, contracts, and oaths have an even more important place on the level of the sovereign-subject relationship. Grotius is in agreement with many jurists who maintained that these moral principles derive their strength from the law of mankind, and not from the civil laws. According to the former law, subjects have the right to free themselves from their con tracts with a ruler whose actions lead either to damage or to a public disaster.

Grotius argues that, on the level of state relationships, treaties must be observed in peace and in war. Thus, the law of mankind provides specific precepts in all human relationships. To observe these means to confirm the dictum: *Pacta sunt servanda.*

NOTES

1. Supra, 3-5.

2. Grotius uses the term "essential traits." See Supra, 6.

3. *J.Pr.*, 8. The sets of rules and precepts of law, known as "Dogmatica" are found in Grotius' work *De Jure Praedae Commentarius*, *J.Pr.*, 8-30.

4. *J. B.P.* , i. I. 14. I.

5. *J.Pr.*, 13.

6. *J.B.P.*, ii. 5. 9. 3.

7. Ibid., i. 2. 8. 10.

8. Ibid., i. 2. 8. 3. Grotius agrees that Christ advocated patience when personal damage was in question. At the same time, the protection of the innocent demanded that evil be punished by the society. As for the passage quoted above, Grotius contended that Christ spoke to the ordinary men and not to magistrates. The former should be patient with the wrongdoers; the latter must not tolerate evil.

9. Ibid. , i. 4. I. 3..

10. *J.Pr.*, 20.

11. *First, Individual citizens should not only refrain from injuring other citizens, both as a whole and as individuals;*

secondly, Citizens should not only refrain from seizing one another's possessions, whether these be held privately or in common, but should furthermore contribute individually both that which is necessary to other individuals and that which is necessary to the whole. Ibid., 21.

12. *Lex* indicated that the promotion of public well-being implied the promotion of the private well-being. Livi quoted: "while the state remains unharmed, it will easily answer for the safety of private property, too." Ibid., 22, 23.

13. Ibid.,   23.

14. *J. B.P.*, i. 4. 4. I.

15. It is important to note here that Grotius was still in the pre-Lockian tradition and believed that the power of legislation, once delegated to the sovereign, automatically became the sole possession of the sovereign. Modern democratic separation of powers was unknown to him or to his age. Grotius did not separate legislature, executive, and judiciary, as did Montesquieu in a later age, because he was too much taken by the idea of the divine right of kings.

Another bad mistake of Grotius was his view on slavery. Although a great supporter of freedom and equality, he was still under the influence of Aristotle, with whom he agreed on this point.

16. *J.Pr.*, 36.

17. Ibid., 36.

18. *J.B.P.*, i. 4. 7. I.

19. Here is the basis for the international law of Grotius, with its positive form found in pacts and written agreements between states.

20. *J.Pr.*, 26.

21. For Grotius the law of mankind provided the final authority for all states. Yet, aware of the fact that in some cases the statutory laws may be the expression of human will, not in accordance with the will of God, the conflict between states was likely to arise. In such a situation, only the law of mankind or the unwritten law of nations could provide the solution.

22. *J.Pr.*, 28. Two important points must be made here: (1) the idea of an international court either did not occur to Grotius, or he did not consider it worth discussing, since God and Natural law were the only Supreme Judge and Sovereign over the individual states; (2) international law, like any other law must be enforced. Since the state is in the possession of the physical power, international society and its law, being deprived of such power, can act only as moral force in international disputes or conflicts.

23. Supra, 22-23.

24. *J. B.P.*, ii. 23. 34.

25. Ibid., ii. 23. 3. 4.

26. Ibid., ii.15.12.

27. Ibid., ii. 10. 15. 1.

28. "[T]the Gospel has removed all distinction between peoples, and a broader meaning has been given to

the word 'neighbour.' Besides other passages, this is shown by the noteworthy parable of Christ concerning the Samaritan." Ibid., ii. 12. 20. 3.

29. Ibid., ii. 20. 44. 6.

30. Ibid., ii. 11. 4. 1.

CHAPTER V:
THE LAW OF MANKIND AND WAR

The law of mankind demands that peace and justice be maintained in all situations. Thus, this law provides regulations for man-to-man relationships, state-to-citizen relationships, and finally, state-to-state relationships. Analyzing human associations, Grotius finds the same rule applicable: the ties that hold a family together should be extended so that a large number of families live in a state. This same tie of the brotherhood of men should serve as the uniting force holding together the family of nations.

This orderly state of affairs is often disrupted by the negative use of human freedom. Here is the origin of war. For Grotius, war is justifiable only if it is understood as armed coercion by those who obey the law of mankind. Such coercion may be applied to individuals, to groups of individuals, or to commonwealths, whenever their actions are directly opposed to the law of mankind. Armed coercion is applied in order to reestablish the conditions of peace. The individual has the right to protect his life and property, the state must protect the lives and property of its citizens, and the community of states is under the obligation to defend justice and preserve peace for the commonwealth of mankind.

According to Grotius, neither state nor war were in the original design of God. However, while the state remains a necessary institution promoting the common good, war is an institution to be resorted to only in case of dire necessity. Grotius, therefore, made a distinction between aggressive war, waged either for the sake of war or on the ground of unjust causes, and war waged with the intention of coercing the aggressive forces. In the first case, wars must be condemned as evil, while, in the second case, armed coercion used for the purpose of establishing the peace is sanctioned by the law of mankind. This law demands the enforcement of binding duties and requires obedience to justice. In fact, the law of war can be justified only from the point of view that it is an adjunctive law to the substantive law of peace.

For Grotius, just warfare is a process of law, an equivalent to the judicial procedure. The purpose of the judicial procedure is to end the dispute and, if necessary, to impose punishment upon the culprit. Likewise, the purpose of just warfare is to end the war, to punish the wrongdoer, and to arrive at the situation of peace.

There are three main justifiable causes for war: defense from injury, reparation for injury inflicted, and punishment of the culprit. It is obvious that these causes of war result from necessity. Such causes do not contradict the law of mankind, which provides for defense and recovery of rights, and imposes the duty to punish those who disregard the law. Grotius contrasted the just causes with the unjust ones. The two basic unjust causes of war are expediency and fear. All other reasons, whose underlying motives are expediency and fear, cannot be accepted as just. Thus, any sort of imperialism, irrespective of its definition, is condemned alongside wars arising from the greed for glory, for riches, or for the display of power.

Grotius was against wars in principle. He quotes Plutarch: "War is a cruel thing," and then says that "multitudes of evil flow from war." Neither rashness nor doubtful reasons can justify a war. Wars ought to be undertaken only in case of utmost necessity.

The necessity brings about the following occurrences of armed coercion:

> War may be waged by private persons against private persons, as by a traveller against a highwayman; by those who have sovereign power against those who possess like power, as by David against the king of the Ammonites; by private persons against those who have sovereign power, but not over them, as by Abraham against the king of Babylon and his neighbors; and by those who have sovereign power against private persons who are either their subjects, as in the war waged by David against the party of Ishbosheth, or are not their subjects, as in the war waged by the Romans against the pirates.[1]

The analysis of armed coercion can be conducted on three different levels: armed coercion and the individual, armed coercion and the state, and armed coercion and the commonwealth of mankind. The right to apply coercion is given to man by the law of nature, by natural law, and by the Divine Positive law.

Armed Coercion and the Individual

Grotius begins his discussion of coercion with the first principles of nature. According to these principles, coercion is permitted since man instinctively desires to preserve his life and his property, and to protect and defend himself. Yet, right reason, which is "the basis of goodness," allows the use of force only in cases when the peace and security of the society is endangered. The question of self-preservation implies several problems. Grotius presents the solution given by man in his narrow interpretation of the law of nature. Next, he contrasts this solution with the solution which is offered by right and moral reason.

The conflict between the law of nature as conceived by man and the true law as explained by Christ appears in several instances. The former emphasized self-preservation; the latter demanded the preservation of the community.

> And certainly, if we look to nature alone, in nature there is much less regard for society than concern for the preservation of the individual. But the law of love, especially as set forth in the Gospel, which puts consideration for others on a level with consideration for ourselves, clearly does not permit the injuring of the innocent.[2]

Grotius supports his argument by quoting Plato's Laws: ". . . anyone who does not protect another from violence deserves punishment." The Bible also speaks in similar terms, and implicitly demands the punishment of the aggressors. In the first place, the Old Law proclaimed that just punishment will be accorded to the evildoers: "Whoso shedeth man's blood, by man shall his blood be shed."[3]

In the second place, the New Law demands that good be done to the doers of good; but, at the same time, it warned that "All they that take sword shall perish with the sword."[4] As for the defense of one's life, Grotius states that "a man is more admirable who prefers to be killed than the one who kills."

The second instance illustrating the conflict between the law of nature and the law of the Gospel indicates that, according to the former, defense of property implies the right to kill; the latter demands that property be given up when the life of a human being is at stake. Grotius maintains that the life of a robber has greater value than the preservation of the possession.

> That the law of the Gospel demands more of us, I do not doubt. For if Christ bids that a tunic and a cloack

be given up, and Paul, that an unjust loss be endured, . . . how much more do they wish that things also of greater value be relinquished rather than that a man, the image of God, sprung from the same blood as ourselves be killed![5]

In the third place, the law of nature allowed punishment for the sake of vengeance. Here, again, the law of Christ demanded charity and forgiveness. It did not abolish the right to punish, but warned that the wrongdoer be not punished by an equally guilty person: "He that is without sin among you, let him first cast a stone." Grotius contended that evil should not be returned for evil, and on these grounds he considered vengeance unjust. To this effect, Maximus of Tyre is quoted: "He who takes vengeance is more wicked than he who did the wrong."[6] Divine law as stated by Christ forbade vengeance, although the human interpretation of the law of nature permitted it. For Grotius, punishments, whether private or public, were not justifiable if their origin was found in the desire for revenge.

Finally, in all situations and on all levels of authority, individual decisions ought to be in accordance with the dictum: "God is to be obeyed rather than men." The obedience of a man to his conscience is, for Grotius, above all other considerations. This essential element in every human being incorporates both faith and right reason. The two raise man above nature and direct him to God. The example given by Christ is the standard for all men, and especially for the Christians.

That we may honourably neglect the care of our own lives in order that, to the best of our ability, we may safeguard the life and eternal salvation of another. . . . Such conduct is above all becoming for Christians. In this they imitate the most perfect example set by Christ, for He was willing to die for us who were yet ungodly and hostile.[7]

The conflict between natural and moral reason is obvious in the examples quoted above. Natural reason led men's actions towards self-centeredness, which minimized the possibilities of the life in the community. Moral reason suggested greater care for the community than for one's own life. Grotius maintained that adherence to the precepts of moral reason had the advantage of preserving community, which in turn meant the preservation of the individual.

Armed Coercion and the State

The law of nature allowed for the private administration of justice, for private coercion by force, and for private infliction of punishments. This right, the *sui juris*, was freely delegated by the individuals to the state, which now appears as the arbiter in the field of justice. Grotius insisted that this right be practiced with lawfulness, with charity, and with good faith. The state, thus, became empowered with the duty of defending and recovering the rights of individual citizens and with the right of inflicting punishments, including the capital punishment.

As regards the first, Grotius says that coercion by force will be lawful as long as there is violence committed by men who do not allow the lovers of peace to live in peace. Christian princes are, therefore, bidden by the Gospel to secure to other Christians and, in the first place, to their Christian subjects, a tranquil life. This duty often demands that the "multitude of evil doers" be brought to justice. As regards the second, namely, the right to punish, Grotius indicated that the law of the Gospel allowed chastisements, since they left no injury or any loss of reputation. The law of nature and most human laws prescribed capital punishment, but Grotius found that the law of Christ demanded that the Christian should abstain from such condemnations.

Although accepting the fact of the sentence of capital punishment, which was practiced in Christian states,

Grotius quoted an example from the pre-Christian era, thus probably stating his own view on this question:

> Nevertheless, it will be profitable for Christian rulers at least in some measure, to set before themselves for imitation the example of Sabaco, king of Egypt, most famous for his uprightness, who according to Diodorus, changed capital punishments into condemnations to hard labour, with most fortunate results.[8]

The duty of each sovereign is to maintain peace and order in his own state. His duty also implies the protection of the citizens from outside dangers. Thus, a state has the right to resort to armed coercion whenever a foreign state has committed a crime against the law of mankind. Grotius enumerates the main crimes which must be suppressed and, if necessary, punished: first, when a state attacks another without being provoked, when one nation interferes in the affairs of another nation and thus tries to disturb the home rule of a sovereign country, when a state violates a treaty or an alliance, and when a state mistreats ambassadors or the citizens of another state; second, crimes of a similar nature are: the desire to rule others against their will on the pretext that this rule is for their own good, the invasion of the territory of outsiders in a war, and the support of the ruler and the people of a country which is waging an unjust war.

Just wars were confirmed by the consent of all nations. Grotius found this confirmation in Greek and Roman history. This offered proof of the fact that wars were waged for the sake of law and justice. That "the Sacred Scriptures" confirmed the right to wage just wars, Grotius did not doubt.

> But God has commanded that wars be waged, as undertakings congruous with His Will, and has furthermore declared himself to be their Author and Aid. He has even accepted the appelation "the man of war" as appropriate to His own majesty.[9]

Grotius quoted the event at which the high priest Melchizedek assured Abraham that the enemies would be delivered into Abraham's hands, since the cause of Abraham was just. David won victories because he fought "the battles of the Lord." And God Himself prescribed regulations for warfare through Moses, and approved readiness for the defense of justice through John the Baptist.

According to Grotius, the doctrine of a just war applied to Christians whenever the defense of one's own commonwealth was at stake. In fact, the defense of innocents was the duty of a Christian. Although Grotius admitted that the law of Christ commanded abstention from force, he argued that this same law did not explicitly abolish all wars.

> . . . the law of Christ did away with the law of Moses only in respect to the separation of the Gentiles from the Jews. But it by no means did away with the things which are honorable by nature and by the common agreement of the more civilized Gentiles; rather it included them in the general teaching of all that is honourable and virtuous. Now in truth the punishment of crimes, and the use of arms which prevent wrongdoing, are by nature considered praiseworthy.[10]

It has been pointed out that, in accordance with the human law and with the confirmation of the divine law, the statutory law and the sovereign are the final authority for the citizens. A foreign state has no right of intervention in the domestic affairs of another state. Yet, Grotius argued that, from the standpoint of the law of mankind, such interference is permissible and is even the duty of other states whenever there is excessive oppression and tyranny exercised over the citizens by a ruthless ruler. Whenever there is manifest oppression "which smells to high heavens," the bond of humanity demands the protection of the oppressed. Grotius considered such action as a moral obligation, stemming from the fact that man must protect his fellow-man. This obligation is above the power of sovereignty. Its execution accords with the command of the Supreme Sovereign, whose law of mankind stands above the statutory laws of the individual states.

A nation, even if not an ally, when unjustly attacked, should be defended by all who can lend such help. By this action, demanded by the unwritten law of nations, an aggressor must be suppressed. That law embraces all nations and, therefore, all men who participate in the God-established commonwealth of mankind, which is above the men-established individual commonwealths.

Grotius justified neutrality only when interference in a war was likely to bring complete disaster or when such action was going to produce further conflagration for mankind. If a war cannot be isolated and brought to an end, then the innocent party must be protected:

> The third cause for undertaking wars on behalf of others is obligation to friends, to whom aid has not been promised, to be sure, but yet is owed under a certain principle of friendship, if it can be rendered easily and without loss.[11]

For Grotius, obedience to the law of mankind, the common tie of kinship binding on all men, and the express commands of God demanded that wars be waged against those "who commit injustice."

Armed Coercion and the Commonwealth of Mankind

The whole system of Grotius has an underlying assumption: moral laws apply equally to the individual and to the state. There is a potential dynamism in both for the preservation of peace and for the promotion of the common good. Thus, Grotius draws a parallel between the individual and the state, and indicates that the law of mankind grants rights to, and imposes duties on, both. However, the assumption of Grotius is that, with the movement from the law of nature to the human laws, the right of self-preservation tends to be complemented with the duty of the preservation of others. Thus, the duty of a state to protect its citizens is transferred to the family of states, which becomes morally obligated to secure peace and justice for the commonwealth of mankind. Any act of an individual state that is contrary to the law of mankind must, therefore, be corrected by the states that obey this law.

Among the misdemeanors affecting the commonwealth of mankind, Grotius quoted crimes against mankind as a whole. Thus, violating peace conditions and acquiring things which belong to mankind in common, claiming parts of the free sea as one's own territory, hampering or monopolizing lawful navigation and trade, and claiming the territory of uncivilized and heathen peoples are breaches of the law of mankind.

Grotius found that the precepts of a universal religion and the precepts of the law of mankind have the basic elements of identity in themselves. Since the Christian religion commanded peace and justice, Grotius saw in its spread the dynamic movement of the law of mankind, which was likely to bring men and nations closer to one another.

He considered a crime every attempt to obstruct the peaceful advance of this process.[12] The cruel treatment of the Christians by the non-Christian rulers was another crime against which the law of mankind demanded intervention.

> Constantine took up arms against Maxentius and Licinius, and other Roman emperors either took up arms against the Persians, or threatened to do so, unless these should check their persecutions of the Christians on account of their religion.[13]

Grotius found discrepancies with the law of mankind in two more instances. First, Dante's idea of the universal state was not acceptable. Grotius opposed the creation of an universal empire, thereby rejecting the possibility of a world state.

> Nor should any one be influenced by the arguments of Dante, by which he strives to prove that such a right [of ruling over even the most distant and hitherto unknown peoples] belongs to the Emperor because that is advantageous for the human race. The advantages which it brings are in fact offset by its disadvantages. For as a ship may attain to such a size that it cannot be steered, so also the number of inhabitants and the distance between places may be so great as not to tolerate a single government.[14]

Second, Grotius attacked the claim of the pope to universal rulership. The Papal Donation,[15] which granted certain areas of the world to Spain and to Portugal, was not in accordance with the law of mankind. The Donation hampered free trade, freedom of the seas, and had direct unfavourable effects on the uncivilized peoples. Grotius demanded that the law of mankind be freely accepted and not forcibly imposed upon all the nations of the world.[16]

After discussing the causes of armed coercion, and after defining the just and unjust war, Grotius undertook the presentation of the various methods used in the application of armed coercion. His contention was that, once the war has been started, the most efficient methods should be used to bring it to an end.

In dealing with this problem, Grotius presents the actual usages in war.[17] These methods were in accordance with the so-called law of nations which he found in his study of history. The *jus gentium* and the custom "which has brought law beneath its sway" provided the rules of warfare widely accepted by many nations. Thus, this law provided for rights in terms of human justice.

The law of war permitted killing of enemies, bodily violence, devastations, looting, and acquisition of objects owned by the enemy. This same law gave full right over the captives, and the right of rulership over the conquered peoples. Thus, all subjects of the enemy, whether soldiers or civilians, had to bear the consequences of war. This rule of license to kill, to harm, and to injure has been applied to infants, women, and prisoners. Neither the supplicants, nor the persons whose unconditional surrender had been accepted, could rely on the hope that their lives would be saved. The practice of killing hostages was also generally accepted as lawful by most nations. The same law of nations, based on practices and customs, allowed destruction and plunder of enemy property. Since the victors in a war had the right to kill the captives, their right to loot and pillage was valid, even in cases in which the enemy had surrendered. The looting included the dedicated and sacred things.

The acquiring of ownership over objects and persons constitutes the second group of rights to which the nations engaged in a war are entitled. However, the conqueror should be allowed to acquire only that amount which is equivalent to the amount of things owned. In accordance with this rule, the forcible acquisition of enemy property was allowed.[18] The *ius gentium* allowed the storming of a city that had rejected peace. It also allowed the acquisition of all movable goods. The right of ownership over things did not differ from the right of ownership over persons. The law of war also permitted the assumption of governing power over the conquered peoples, and the subjugation and even complete extermination of states.

As a contrast to these crude provisions of warfare, Grotius presented his famous moderations.[19] He demanded that irrational methods used in war be corrected and moderated by considerations of right reason, inner justice, and Christian charity. The considerations of utility also suggested moderate action in war.

But we must keep in mind that which we have re-
called elsewhere also, that the rules of love are broader than the rules of law. . . .

Nevertheless virtue itself, in low esteem in the
present age, ought to forgive me if, when of itself it
is despised, I cause it to be valued on account of its
advantages.[20]

Taking these two propositions as the guide for right reason and charity, Grotius tried to define the methods of warfare which the unwritten law of nations allowed. According
to this law, applicable to all men and all nations, warfare
had no place among the useful arts. Therefore, all harsh provisions connected with waging a war must be regarded as
permissions and not as rights.

To the rules of warfare established by custom, Grotius
applied qualifications derived from the unwritten law
of mankind. Humanity and justice demand that only the
wrongdoers be punished. Thus, the punishment may be justifiable only if it is the punishment for a wrong directly committed by an individual.

No one can justly be killed intentionally, except as a
just penalty or in case we are able in no other way to
protect our life and property; although the killing of a
man on account of transitory things, even if it is not at
variance with justice in a strict sense, nevertheless is
not in harmony with the law of love.[21]

The right to kill an enemy applies only as long as the
immediate danger is present. Once the enemy is subdued
and his ability to harm is removed, right and godly action
should direct us to show mercy even to the guilty. There is
no justification for the punishment of innocent people, even
though they are subjects of the enemy state. Once the vic-
tory has been achieved, doing harm to the enemy becomes

a matter of vengeance, of the display of one's power, or of the exercise of uncontrolled anger. Grotius condemns actions originating in these motives, and rejects them since they are both un-Christian and inhuman. Although, strictly speaking, this is the right of the victor, "to let go one's full right is an act of mercy." Thus, moral justice, which here appears as the opposite of human justice, demands that supplicants be judged in accordance with the heaviness of their errors. The instigators of war must be treated differently from their followers. To spare captives must be considered as a rule of the universal law. That women and children must be spared is indisputable, for Grotius. Likewise, people who are engaged in preserving peace and who are opposed to warmaking should not suffer the consequences of war. In this group belong priests, monks, novices; men of letters and workers on the land; and merchants and artisans.

The right to kill an enemy in a war extended to the right of killing hostages. Grotius condemned such practices:

> It is then, not to be wondered at if we read that hostages who were personally guiltless were put to death for a wrong done by their state, either as though done by their individual consent, or by the public consent in which their own was included. But now that a truer knowledge has taught us that lordship over life is reserved for God, it follows that no one by his individual consent can give to another a right over life, either his own life, or that of a fellow citizen.[22]

There is usually no reason for devastation of a country, except if by this method the enemy is forced to sue for peace. Grotius condemns looting and destruction of enemy territory as the manifestation of greed, ferocity, vengeance, and irrationality. Utility itself indicates that fields and agricultural land ought to be preserved. Abstention from looting towns and devastating the countryside is a sign of confidence in one's own strength. The only result which the opposite action may produce is the hatred and despair of the population.

Grotius argued that it is against nature that human beings should be slaves, but, at the same time, he maintained that slavery may be imposed through an act of human will. Although in agreement with Aristotle as far as the theory of slavery was concerned, Grotius departs from the *ius gentium*, which advocated slavery. He indicated that the practices of the Jews, of the Christians, and of the Mohammedans were far above the practices of the Romans.

The treatment of conquered peoples requires justice and clemency. The victor in a just war has the right to punish the guilty and to recover debts incurred before and during the war. The situation of peace will be maintained if the conqueror is moderate in his demands. "Let this be a new method of conquering, to fortify ourselves with mercy and generosity."[23]

Salust says of the ancient Romans: "Our ancestors, being most scrupulous of persons, used to deprive the vanquished of nothing save the power to do harm." This is a view which could worthily have been uttered by a Christian; and with it accords another sentence of the same writer: "Wise men wage war to secure peace, and endure toil in the hope of ease."[24]

Grotius suggests the best method for maintaining peace with a conquered nation: actions of the victor must be based on the principles of justice. In other words, the victorious nation should extend equal rights to the conquered nation. Grotius offers the example given by the emperor Antonius, by whose decree all inhabitants of the Roman world became citizens of Rome.

Wisdom and humanity will lead the victor to the following treatment of conquered peoples: first, the vanquished should be given the right of retaining their own governing power, as long as there is some provision for the security of the victors; second, an attempt to harmonize systems of government should be made; third, there should be no effort to change the local customs; fourth, except when the religion is false, the right of the conquered to practice their ancestral religion should be granted. The above analysis clearly indicates that the strong elements stemming from Christian convictions of Grotius are easily detected. The presentation of the actual methods of warfare compared with his quest for their alteration strikingly point to this fact. Grotius believed that the law of mankind firmly rested on the universal principles of goodness, charity, high-mindedness, good faith, and moderation. Since, for him, every just war was waged for the preservation of these principles, he contended that the return to the conditions of peace was only possible through the application of these principles in all armed coercions.

NOTES

1. *J.B.P.*, i. 4. I. I.

2. Ibid., ii. I. 4. 2.

3. *J. Pr.*, p. 98.

4. Ibid., p. 36.

5. *J.B.P.*, ii. I. 13. 1.

6. Ibid., ii. 20. 12. 3.

7. Ibid., ii. 24. I.

8. Ibid., ii. 20. 12. 3.

9. *J. Pr.*, p. 35.

10. *J. B.P.* i. 2. 7. 14.

11. Ibid., ii. 15. 5.

12. "For as the matter of first importance the kingdom of heaven is to be sought, that is the spread of the Gospel." Ibid., ii. 15. II. 2.

13. Ibid. , ii. 25. 8. 2.

14. Ibid. , ii. 22. xiii. I.

15. *M.L.*, pp. 15-18.

16. "For even if something is advantageous for any one, the right is not conferred upon me to impose this upon him by force. For those who have the use of their reason ought to have free choice of what is advantageous or not advantageous." *J.B.P.*, ii. 22. 12.

17. Ibid., iii. 4-9.

18. Grotius quoted the case of Abraham and the five kings to indicate that God approved of the right of pillage within the natural limits. Ibid., iii. 6. I. I.

19. Ibid., iii. 11-16.

20. Ibid., iii. 13. 4. 1; iii. 12. 8. 1.

21. Ibid., iii. 11. 2.

22. Ibid., iii. 11. 18. 1.

23. Grotius gave this dictum of Caesar the dictator as the example of good statesmanship. Ibid., iii. 15. 12. 2.

24. Ibid., iii. 16. 2. 1.

CONCLUSION

Grotius belongs to the tradition of natural law theory. In fact, he is often designated as the founder of modern natural law theory. Yet, this statement allows for two different interpretations. In the first place, from the point of view of philosophy, the merit of Grotius consists in the fact that he systematically separated the philosophical from the theological elements in that theory.[1] In this respect, he may be regarded as an innovator whose purpose was to discard the latter elements in order to preserve the former. Judged from this standpoint, Grotius belongs to the school of rationalist international theory. In the second place, and from the standpoint of theology, the significance of Grotius is much greater. He may be regarded as the expounder of the Christian philosophy of law and of Christian interpretation of international theory, since he determined the proper relationship between the natural law (or law of nature) theory and Divine Positive law.[2]

According to Grotius, man participates in a dynamic process of acquiring the knowledge of the purpose of his existence. This dynamism implies degrees of understanding. Thus, the division offered by Grotius indicates that the knowledge of propositions as derived in the theory of natural law has to be complemented and superseded by the knowledge of the precepts of Divine Positive law. It is plain that

Grotius contrasted the natural law with Divine Positive law in order to indicate that human actions ought to be adjusted to a higher level of man's potentialities. Grotius stated that the law of Christ defines the will of God. He implied that this law ought to be accepted as the law of mankind. The Christian ethic, being the "nearest perfection," becomes, therefore, the goal of human strivings, not only for the sake of creating conditions of the "good life," but also as the *telos* of human existence. Thus, the ethic of Grotius is not an end in itself, but a dynamic movement towards an ideal. The achievement of the ideal presented by the moral code of Christ is impossible by human efforts only. The theory of Grotius, therefore, necessarily implies the need for grace and for the immanence of God in the world.

The precepts of the Christian ethic, as explained by Grotius, are equally applicable to an individual and to the family of nations. Just as the individual is a unit in himself, the state is also "a self-sufficient aggregation." However, both the individual and the state must relate themselves to other units, both in the particular and in the universal community. Personal ethics, then, must not be different from international ethics.

The system of ethics, and primarily of Christian ethics, is dominant in Grotius. Hence, the evaluation of his international theory remains one-sided if the ethical precepts guiding that theory are ignored. Grotius emphasized the dual nature of man, according to which man can exercise positive or negative freedom. The same definition as regards the use of freedom is applicable to the states, which can either cooperate with or can appear as the opponents of one another. Grotius contends that freedom must be used positively, that is to say, in accordance with the law of mankind. The nature of international society demands peace, justice, and cooperation among states, "since we are born for a life of fellowship." Justice in the international society is maintained primarily through the observance of the unwritten law of nations.

Grotius rejects power politics as a means of foreign policy on the grounds of its diametrical opposition to universal justice. The law of mankind favors the equality of all states and provides for the harmony of national interests. War is allowed only as a means for the coercion and for the due punishment of delinquent states. The application of such coercion is, in most cases, obligatory on the commonwealth of mankind. For Grotius, history has a significance insofar as it represents major or minor periods in which man has achieved approximations to the law of mankind. Hence, in the eyes of Grotius, history is not seen as linear progress, although a potentiality for movement upwards does exist.

The influence of Grotius on human thought has been of a lasting value. His basic propositions remain the necessary requirements for the international order. With his law of peace, he presented to the world the ideal conception of a family of nations, united under the Sovereignty of God, in a common wealth of mankind. Thus, Grotius must be regarded as one of the chief expounders of the basic ideals that are contained in documents like the League of Nations Covenant, the United Nations Charter, and the United Nations Declaration of Human Rights.

NOTES

1. Supra, 11, n. 1.

2. See Supra, 6, 7

DEFINITION OF TERMS

Divine law	Ontological source of all law; perfect and dynamic law flowing from God's Being; never completely disclosed to man.
Natural law	Ontological law flowing from the Reason of God; perfect and dynamic coordinator of God's Creativity and of God 's Will.
The true law of nature	Ontological law directed by God's Creativity; perfect and dynamic law sustaining the universe and all created matter.
Divine Positive law	Ontological law defining God's Will; given by God to the Hebrews, and by Christ to mankind; defined in the Old and in the New Testament; the indispensable link between God and man; its dynamism expounded by the church.
The natural law	Ontological law defining God's Will; given by God to the Hebrews, and by Christ to mankind; defined in the Old and in the New Testament; the indispensable link between God and man; its dynamism expounded by the church.

Modern theory of natural law	Rationalist theory dealing with moral actions of man; based on human reason and not implying the existence of God.
The law of nature	Descriptive scientific laws guiding the irrational beings and created matter; partial derivation from the true law of nature.
The law of mankind	The universal law applicable to all men and to all nations; in Grotius, the unwritten or primary law of nations.
The law of nations	The secondary law of nations, defined in written agreements and pacts between groups of states; also, the *jus gentium* and practices of states in their relationships, based on the established custom.
The municipal law	Statutory law binding on all members of a municipality.
The state law	Statutory law binding on all citizens of a state.
Unrevealed Divine law	The law found in nature indicating the existence of a Supreme Being.
Revealed Divine law	Divine Positive law, presenting the express commands of God given in the Old and in the New Testament.

Freedom of God	Perfect and unlimited, dynamically directed towards good.
The freedom of man	Imperfect and dual in its character; directed either toward God or toward nature; the potential origin of evil.
God's creation	The created world as seen by man.
The moral reason of man	The guide for moral action; leads into proper understanding of the relationship between self-love and the love for others.
The natural reason of man	The nature-oriented reason emphasizing the self-love at the expense of the love for others; insists on self-preservation, even at the expense of the preservation of others.

BIBLIOGRAPHY

Primary Sources

Grotius, Hugo. *De Jure Belli ac Pacis Libri Tres*. Trans. by Francis W. Kelsey. Oxford: Clarendon Press, 1925.

—. *The Law of War and Peace*. Trans. by Louise R. Loomis. New York: Walter J. Black, 1949.

—. *De Jure Praedae, Commentary on the Law of Prize and Booty*. Oxford: Clarendon Press, 1950.

—. *Mare Liberum, The Freedom of the Seas or the Right Which Belongs to the Dutch to Take Part in the East Indian Trade*. Trans. by R. V. D. Magoffin. New York: Oxford University Press, 1916.

—. *The Introduction to Dutch Jurisprudence*. London: Charles Herbert, 1845.

—. *Hugonis Grotti Annotata ad Vetus Testamentum*. . . . (Lutetiae Parisiorum, sumptibus S. et G. Gramosy, 1644).

—. *Hugonis Grotti Annotationem in Novum Testamentum tomus secundus* (Parisus, sumptibus authoris et prostant exemplaria apud viduam G. Pele, 1646).

—. *Veritate Religionis Christianae, The Truth of the Christian Religion in Six Books*. Trans. by John Clarke. Cambridge, UK: J. Hall and Son, 1860.

Secondary Sources

Beach, Waldo, and H. Richard Niebuhr. *Christian Ethics.* New York: Ronald Press, 1955.

Corvin, Edward S. "The 'Higher Law' Background of American Constitutional Law." *Harvard Law Review* 27, no. 2 (1928): 149-85.

Dekker, E. D. "Deism." In Volume 5, *Encyclopedia of the Social Sciences.* E.D. Seligman, ed. New York: Macmillan, 1931.

D'Entreves, Alexander Passerin. *Natural Law.* London: Hutchinson University Library, 1951.

Foster, Michael B. *Masters of Political Thought: Plato to Machiavelli.* New York: Houghton Mifflin, 1941.

Fruin, Robert M. "An Unpublished Work of Hugo Grotius." *Biblioteca Visseriana,* Volume 5. E. J. Brill: Lugduni Batavorum Apud, 1925.

Harding, Arthur L. *Origins of the Natural Law Tradition.* Volume 1. Dallas: South Methodist Press, 1954.

—. *Natural Law and Natural Rights.* Volume 2. Dallas: South Methodist Press, 1955.

—. *Religion, Morality and Law.* Volume 3. Dallas: South Methodist Press, 1955.

Knight, William Stanley Macbean. *The Life and Works of Hugo Grotius.* London: The Grotius Society Publications (No. 4), 1925.

Kosters, J. "Les Fondements du Droit des Gens." *Biblioteca Viseriana,* Volume 4. E. J. Brill: Lugduni Batavorum Apud, 1925.

Lawrence, Thomas J. "The Principles of International Law." *The American Journal of International Law* 19 (1925).

Mackintosh, Sir James. *A Study of the Law of Nations and Nature.* London, 1835.

Meulen, Jacob Ter and P.J.J. Diermanse. *Bibliographie des Ecrits Imprimes de Hugo Grotius.* LaHaye: Martinus Nijhoff, 1950.

Niebuhr, Reinhold. *An Interpretation of Christian Ethics.* New York: Harper and Bros., 1935.

Nussbaum, Arthur. *A Concise History of the Law of Nations*. New York: Macmillan, 1954.

Pound, A. "Philosophical Theory and International Law." *Biblioteca Visseriana*, Volume 1. Brill: Lugduni Batavorum Apud, 1925.

Ramsey, Paul. *Basic Christian Ethics*. New York: Charles Scribner's Sons, 1950.

Rutherford, T. *Institutes of Natural Law; Course of Lectures on Grotius' "De Jure Belli ac Pacis."* Baltimore : W. J. Neal, 1832.

Sabine, G. H. *A History of Political Theory*. New York: Holt, 1937.

Strauss, Leo. *Natural Right and History*. Chicago: The University of Chicago Press, 1953.

Van Vollenhoven, Cornelis. *The Framework of Grotius' Book "De Jure Belli ac Pacis (1625)."* Verhandelingen der Koninklijke Akademie van Wetenschappen. Amsterdam: Noord-Hollandsche Uitgevers Maatschappij, 1931.

—. *The Three Stages in the Evolution of the Law of Nations*. The Hague: M. Nijhoff, 1919.

Vreeland, Hamilton. *Hugo Grotius the Father of the Modern Science of International Law*. New York: Oxford University Press, 1917.

Wild, John. *Plato's Modern Enemies and the Theory of Natural Law*. Cambridge: Harvard University Press, 1953.

Wright, Benjamin F. *American Interpretations of Natural Law*. Cambridge: Harvard University Press, 1931.

Wright, Quincy. The Study of International Relations. New York: Appleton-Century-Crofts, 1955.

—. *A Study of War*. Chicago: The University of Chicago Press, 1953.

List of Grotius' Works (in chronological order)
Adamus Exul (*The Exile of Adam*; tragedy). The Hague, 1601
De Republica Emendanda (*To Improve the Dutch Republic*; manuscript 1601). The Hague, 1984

Parallelon Rerumpublicarum (*Comparison of Constitutions*; manuscript 1601-02). Haarlem, 1801-03.

De Indis (*On the Indies*; manuscript 1604-05). (Pub. 1868 as *De Jure Praedae. Commentary on the Law of Prize and Booty*, ed. Martine Julia van Ittersum. Liberty Fund, 2006.

Christus Patiens (*The Passion of Christ*; tragedy). Leiden, 1608.

Mare Liberum (*On the Freedom of the Seas*; from chapter 12 of *De Indis*). Leiden, 1609.

De Antiquitate Reipublicae Batavicae (*On the Antiquity of the Batavian Republic*). Leiden, 1610.

Meletius (Manuscript 1611). Leiden, 1988

Meletius. Ed. G.H.M. Posthumus Meyjes. Brill, 1988.

Annales et Historiae de Rebus Belgicus (*Annals and History of the Low Countries*; manuscript 1612). Amsterdam, 1657

The Annals and History of the Low-Countrey-Warres. Ed. Thomas Manley. London, 1665.

Ordinum Hollandiae ac Westfrisiae Pietas (*The Piety of the States of Holland and Westfriesland*). Leiden, 1613.

De Imperio Summarum Potestatum Circa Sacra (*On the Power of Sovereigns Concerning Religious Affairs*; manuscript 1614-17). Paris, 1647.

De Satisfactione Christi Adversus Faustum Socinum (*On the Satisfaction of Christ Against [the doctrines of] Faustus Socinus*). Leiden, 1617

Defensio Fidei Catholicae de Satisfactione Christi (*Defense of Catholic Faith of Christian Satisfaction*). Ed. Edwin Rabbie. van Gorcum, 1990.

Inleydinge tot de Hollandsche Rechts-geleertheit (*Introduction to Dutch Jurisprudence*; written in Loevenstein). The Hague, 1631.

Bewijs van den Waaren Godsdienst (*Proof of the True Religion*). Rotterdam, 1622

Apologeticus (Defense of the actions which led to his arrest). Paris, 1922.

De Jure Belli ac Pacis. Paris, 1625.

De Veritate Religionis Christianae (*On the Truth of the Christian Religion*). Paris, 1627.

Sophompaneas (Joseph; tragedy). Amsterdam, 1635.

De Origine Gentium Americanarum Dissertatio (*Dissertation of the Origin of the American Peoples*). Paris 1642.

Via ad Pacem Ecclesiasticam (*The Way to Religious Peace*). Paris, 1642

Annotationes in Vetus Testamentum (*Commentaries on the Old Testament*). Amsterdam, 1644.

Annotationes in Novum Testamentum (*Commentaries on the New Testament*). Amsterdam and Paris, 1641–50

De Fato (*On Destiny*). Paris, 1648.

Suggested Further Reading

Since 1957, when this text was submitted in partial fulfillment of the Master's degree at the University of Chicago, numerous scholars have contributed to our understanding of Grotius and his work. The following is a partial list of sources suggested for further study on the subject.

Blom, Hans W. *Property, Piracy and Punishment: Hugo Grotius on War and Booty in "De Jure Praedae" – Concepts and Contexts*. Brill Academic Pub, 2009.

Borschberg, Peter. *Hugo Grotius: "Commentarius in Theses XI."* Berne: Peter Lang, 1994.

—. "Hugo Grotius' Theory of Trans-Oceanic Trade Regulation: Revisiting *Mare Liberum (1609)*." *Itinerario* 29 (2005): 31-53.

Bozeman, Adda. "On the Relevance of Hugo Grotius and *De Jure Belli ac Pacis* For Our Times." *Grotiana* 1, no. 1 (1980): 65-124.

Brett, Annabel. "Natural Right and Civil Community: The Civil Philosophy of Hugo Grotius." *The Historical Journal* 45, no. 1 (2002): 31-51.

Butler, Charles. *The Life of Hugo Grotius With Brief Minutes of the Civil, Ecclesiastical, and Literary History of the Netherlands*. Middlesex, UK: Echo Library, 2007.

Cerny, Gerald. *Hugo Grotius: "Meletius sive de iis quae inter Christianos Conveniunt Epistola."* Trans. by Guillaume HM Posthumus Meyjes. *Studies in the History of Christian Thought* 40. Leiden: EJ Brill, 1988.

Chroust, Anton-Herman. "Hugo Grotius and the Scholastic Natural Law Tradition." *The New Scholasticism* 17, no. 2 (2008): 101-33.

de Araujo, Marcelo. "Hugo Grotius, Contractualism, and the Concept of Private Property: An Institutionalist Interpretation." *History of Philosophy Quarterly* 26, no. 4 (2009): 353-71.

Edwards, Charles S. *Hugo Grotius, the Miracle of Holland: A Study in Political and Legal Thought.* Nelson-Hall, 1981.

Greene, William. "The Miracle of Holland: Hugo Grotius: Naturalist, Eclectic, or Theonomist?" *The Preterist Archive*, March 30, 2005. Last accessed April 4, 2013, http://www.preteristarchive.com/StudyArchive/g/grotius-hugo.html

Haakonssen, Knud. "Hugo Grotius and the History of Political Thought." *Political Theory* 13, no. 2 (1985): 239-65.

Haskell, John. "Hugo Grotius in the Contemporary Memory of International Law: Secularism, Liberalism, and the Politics of Restatement and Denial." *Emory International Law Review* 25, no. 1 (2011).

Heering, Jan Paul. *Hugo Grotius as Apologist for the Christian Religion: A Study of His Work "De Veritate Religionis Christianae, 1640."* Vol. 111. Leiden: Brill, 2004.

Ittersum, Martine Julia van. *Profit and Principle: Hugo Grotius, Natural Rights Theories and the Rise of Dutch Power in the East Indies: 1595-1615.* Leiden: Brill, 2006.

Keene, Edward. *Beyond the Anarchical Society: Grotius, Colonialism and Order in World Politics.* Cambridge University Press, 2002.

Lesaffer, Randall. "On Roman Ethics, Rhetoric and Law in Grotius: Hugo Grotius und die Antike. Romisches Recht und Romische Ethik im Fruhneuzeitlichen Naturrecht,

Benjamin Straumann." *Journal of the History of International Law* 10 (2008): 343.

MacDougal, Myres. *The Public Order of the Oceans: A Contemporary International Law of the Sea.* New Haven: Yale University Press, 1962.

—, Harold Dwight Lasswell, and Ivan A. Vlasic. *Law and Public Order in Space.* New Haven: Yale University Press, 1963.

Newman, Jane O. "Race, Religion, and the Law: Rhetorics of Sameness and Difference in the Work of Hugo Grotius." *Rhetoric and Law in Early Modern Europe* (2001).

Ōnuma, Yasuaki. *A Normative Approach to War: Peace, War, and Justice in Hugo Grotius.* Oxford University Press, 1993.

Porras, Ileana M. "Constructing International Law in the East Indian Seas: Property, Sovereignty, Commerce and War in Hugo Grotius' *De Jure Praedae* — The Law of Prize and Booty, or on How to Distinguish Merchants from Pirates." *Brooklyn Journal of International Law* 31 (2005): 741.

Roberts, Michael B. "Genesis Chapter 1 and Geological Time from Hugo Grotius and Marin Mersenne to William Conybeare and Thomas Chalmers (1620–1825)." *Geological Society, London, Special Publications* 273, no. 1 (2007): 39-49.

Salter, John. "Hugo Grotius: Property and Consent." *Political Theory* 29, no. 4 (2001): 537-55.

—. "Sympathy with the Poor: Theories of Punishment in Hugo Grotius and Adam Smith." *History of Political Thought* 20, no. 2 (1999): 205-24.

Stumpf, Christoph A. *The Grotian Theology of International Law: Hugo Grotius and the Moral Foundations of International Relations.* Vol. 44. Berlin: de Gruyter, 2006.

Tuck, Richard. *The Rights of War and Peace: Political Thought and the International Order From Grotius to Kant.* Clarendon Press, 1999.

Van Ittersum, Martine Julia. "Hugo Grotius in Context: Van Heemskerck's Capture of the Santa Catarina and its

Justification in *De Jure Praedae* (1604-1606)." *Asian Journal of Social Science* 31, no. 3 (2003): 511-548.

Vollenhoven, Cornelius van. "Grotius and Geneva." *Bibliotheca Visseriana*, Vol. V. Leiden: Brill, 1925.

Wilson, Eric Michael. *The Savage Republic: "De Indis" of Hugo Grotius, Republicanism and Dutch Hegemony Within the Early Modern World-System (c. 1600-1619).* Leiden: Brill, 2008.

Yamauchi, Susumu. "The Ambivalence of Hugo Grotius: State Sovereignty and Common Interests of Mankind." *Hitotsubashi Journal of Law and Politics* 22 (1994): 1-17.

Zemanek, Karl. "Was Hugo Grotius Really in Favour of the Freedom of the Seas?" *Journal of the History of International Law* 1 (1999): 48.

APPENDIX

Couldert Brothers
Attorneys and Counsellors at Law
Pan American Building
200 Park Avenue
New York, NY 10017
November 15, 1966

Dear Mr. Sotirovich,

I apologize for having delayed the acknowledgment of receipt of your letter of October 4, 1966, to which you were so kind to attach some pages of your M.A. thesis on Hugo Grotius. I read them with great interest. You went into a problem of whose existence I knew, but of whose substance I am pretty ignorant. Namely, I am pretty familiar with the work of Grotius as one of an international jurist, but my knowledge is, unfortunately, extremely limited concerning Grotius as a Scholar of Divinity and of Divine Law; and I feel that a correct and complete picture of Grotius can be obtained only if those two facets of the same scholar can be brought into focus, and not if they be split into two halves, and one-half be examined without taking notice of the other one, as is normally done by our historians of International Law. In a general way, it is now days too much forgotten to what extend [*sic*] International Law, as to its origin, is indebted to Theology and Divinity Sciences. All this had made that the pages of your Master Degree Thesis you sent me, were for me most interesting, and I hope that in a not too distant future, I will have the privilege to hear more from you on the entire subject matter covered by your thesis.

. . .

Sincerely Yours,

Dr. I. Soubbotitch

INDEX

Abraham, 85, 90, 100n.18
Abuse of freedom, 2, 4
Action, freedom of, 5, 22, 62, 67
Actions of men, 3, 42
Aggressor, punishment of, 86
Alliances, 63, 75 *See also* Treaties, 63, 75
Ally, 91
Althusius, 12 n.1
Ambassadors, inviolability of, 73
Ammonites, king of, 85
Angelic Doctor, 71
Animals, awareness of universe, 19
    sacrifices of, 40
Antonius, emperor, 97
Apostles, 67
Aquinas, St. Thomas, 4, 7, 13 n.5, 71
Archons, *See also* Magistrates, 69
Argument, consent of all nations, 19, 89
    cosmological, 21
Aristotle, 7, 14 n.16, 22, 80, 97
    definition of love, 22
Armed coercion, 83-85, 91, 93

Assemblies of men, 68
Athanasius, St., 7
Atheism, rejection of, 11
Augustine, St., 7

Babylon, king of, 85
Bible, xxvi, 86
    Book of Ecclesiastes, 70
    Genesis, 27 n.12
    Hosea, 38
    Isaiah, 35
    Jeremiah, 38
    Matthew, 66
    Micah, 38
    Psalms, 38
Blessings, enumeration of, 22
Bond of humanity, 90

Caesar, 69, 100 n.23
Causation, chain of, 19
Ceremonies, 38
Charity, Christian, 94
Charter, of the United Nations, xvi, 103

119

Governmental theory, 20
Grace, the need for, 102
Greek and Roman history, 89
Greeks, 40, 66

Harmony, of national interests, 103
    of universe, ix, 21
Hebrews, 36, 38, 74, 105
Hegel, 13
History, bearing of upon law, xiii
    of mankind, 19, 42-43
      God's participation in, 20
      Greek and Roman, 89
      role of, 41
Holy Writ, 74
Honor, 40
Hope, 39, 41, 94, 97
Hosea, 38, *See also* Bible
Hostages, 94, 96
Human existence, 102
    society, 22, 24, 35, 61, 64, 67, 77
Human laws, 17, 62
    precepts of, 67
Human rights, United Nations
    Declaration, 103
Humanity, bond of, 90
Humility, 40

Idea of universal state of Dante, 93
Ills, enumeration of, 22
Image of God, man as, 87
Immanence of God, 102
Immortality of the soul, 37
Imperialism, 84
Importance of miracles, 20
Individual consent, 96
    preservation of, 86

Industry, 64
Inevitability of death, 33
Injustice, condemning, 25
Instigators of war, 96
Institutes of Natural Law, 111
International Law, principles of,
    110
International Relations, study of,
    111
Interpretation, of Christian ethics,
    110
    of God's Will, 43
    of Law of Nature, 31-32, 85-87
    of sacrifice, 37
International ethics, 102
International Order, 103, 115
The Introduction to Dutch
    Jurisprudence, 109
Inviolability of ambassadors, 73
Isaiah, 35, See *also* Bible
Ius, 28
Ius gentium, 94, 97

Jefferson, Thomas, 9
Jeremiah, 38. *See also* Bible
Jesus of Nazareth, 41
Jewish, law, 66. *See also* Law
    Hebraic
    kings, 69
    practices, 38
    tradition, 43
    sacrifices, 39
Judge, supreme, 81
Justice, defense of, 75
    maintenance of, 76
    immutable, 77
    source of, 24

www.ingramcontent.com/pod-product-compliance
Lightning Source LLC
Chambersburg PA
CBHW070914290526
45795CB00001B/311